Primary Bible Reader

Selected KJV passages for young readers

Miriam Howell, *editor*
William Mayhew, Jr., *designer*
Brian Jekel, *illustrator*

A Beka Book
A MINISTRY OF
PENSACOLA CHRISTIAN COLLEGE
PENSACOLA, FLORIDA 32523-9160

Second Edition

Copyright © 1995, 1977 Pensacola Christian College
All rights reserved. Printed in U.S.A. 1999

The Old Testament

THE CREATION

God Made Light
Genesis 1:1–5

In the beginning God created the heaven and the earth.

And the earth was without form, and void; and darkness *was* upon the face of the deep. And the spirit of God moved upon the face of the waters.

And God said, Let there be light: and there was light.

And God saw the light, that *it was* good: and God divided the light from the darkness.

And God called the light Day, and the darkness he called Night. And the evening and the morning were the first day.

God Made Heaven
Genesis 1:6-8

And God said, Let there be a firmament in the midst of the waters, and let it divide the waters from the waters.

And God made the firmament, and divided the waters which *were* under the firmament from the waters which *were* above the firmament: and it was so.

And God called the firmament Heaven. And the evening and the morning were the second day.

God Made Earth
Genesis 1:9–13

And God said, Let the waters under the heaven be gathered together unto one place, and let the dry *land* appear: and it was so.

And God called the dry *land* Earth; and the gathering together of the waters called he Seas: and God saw that *it was* good.

And God said, Let the earth bring forth grass, the herb yielding seed, *and* the fruit tree yielding fruit after his kind, whose seed *is* in itself, upon the earth: and it was so.

And the earth brought forth grass, *and* herb yielding seed after his kind, and the tree yielding fruit, whose seed *was* in itself, after his kind: and God saw that *it was* good.

And the evening and the morning were the third day.

God Made the Sun, Moon, and Stars
Genesis 1:14–19

And God said, Let there be lights in the firmament of the heaven to divide the day from the night; and let them be for signs, and for seasons, and for days, and years:

And let them be for lights in the firmament of the heaven to give light upon the earth: and it was so.

And God made two great lights; the greater light to rule the day, and the lesser light to rule the night: *he made* the stars also.

And God set them in the firmament of the heaven to give light upon the earth,

And to rule over the day and over the night, and to divide the light from the darkness: and God saw that *it was* good.

And the evening and the morning were the fourth day.

God Made the Fish and Birds
Genesis 1:20–23

And God said, Let the waters bring forth abundantly the moving creature that hath life, and fowl *that* may fly above the earth in the open firmament of heaven.

And God created great whales, and every living creature that moveth, which the waters brought forth abundantly, after their kind, and every winged fowl after his kind: and God saw that *it was* good.

And God blessed them, saying, Be fruitful, and multiply, and fill the waters in the seas, and let fowl multiply in the earth.

And the evening and the morning were the fifth day.

God Made Animals and Man
Genesis 1:24–27, 31

And God said, Let the earth bring forth the living creature after his kind, cattle, and creeping thing, and beast of the earth after his kind: and it was so.

And God made the beast of the earth after his kind, and cattle after their kind, and every thing that creepeth upon the earth after his kind: and God saw that *it was* good.

And God said, Let us make man in our image, after our likeness: and let them have dominion over the fish of the sea, and over the fowl of the air, and over the cattle, and over all the earth, and over every creeping thing that creepeth upon the earth.

So God created man in his *own* image, in the image of God created he him; male and female created he them.

And God saw every thing that he had made, and, behold, *it was* very good. And the evening and the morning were the sixth day.

God Rested
Genesis 2:1–3

Thus the heavens and the earth were finished, and all the host of them.

And on the seventh day God ended his work which he had made; and he rested on the seventh day from all his work which he had made.

And God blessed the seventh day, and sanctified it: because that in it he had rested from all his work which God created and made.

ADAM and EVE

The Serpent Comes to Eve

Genesis 3:1–5

Now the serpent was more subtil than any beast of the field which the Lord God had made. And he said unto the woman, Yea, hath God said, Ye shall not eat of every tree of the garden?

And the woman said unto the serpent, We may eat of the fruit of the trees of the garden:

But of the fruit of the tree which *is* in the midst of the garden, God hath said, Ye shall not eat of it, neither shall ye touch it, lest ye die.

And the serpent said unto the woman, Ye shall not surely die:

For God doth know that in the day ye eat thereof, then your eyes shall be opened, and ye shall be as gods, knowing good and evil.

Adam and Eve Sin
Genesis 3:6–15

And when the woman saw that the tree *was* good for food, and that it *was* pleasant to the eyes, and a tree to be desired to make *one* wise, she took of the fruit thereof, and did eat, and gave also unto her husband with her; and he did eat.

And the eyes of them both were opened, and they knew that they *were* naked; and they sewed fig leaves together, and made themselves aprons.

And they heard the voice of the LORD God walking in the garden in the cool of the day: and Adam and his wife hid themselves from the presence of the LORD God amongst the trees of the garden.

And the LORD God called unto Adam, and said unto him, Where *art* thou?

And he said, I heard thy voice in the garden, and I was afraid, because I *was* naked; and I hid myself.

And he said, Who told thee that thou *wast* naked? Hast thou eaten of the tree, whereof I commanded thee that thou shouldest not eat?

And the man said, The woman whom thou gavest *to be* with me, she gave me of the tree, and I did eat.

And the LORD God said unto the woman, What *is* this *that* thou hast done? And the woman said, The serpent beguiled me, and I did eat.

And the LORD God said unto the serpent, Because thou hast done this, thou *art* cursed above all cattle, and above every beast of the field; upon thy belly shalt thou go, and dust shalt thou eat all the days of thy life:

And I will put enmity between thee and the woman, and between thy seed and her seed; it shall bruise thy head, and thou shalt bruise his heel.

NOAH AND THE FLOOD

God Has a Plan
Genesis 6:5–8

And God saw that the wickedness of man *was* great in the earth, and *that* every imagination of the thoughts of his heart *was* only evil continually.

And it repented the LORD that he had made man on the earth, and it grieved him at his heart.

And the LORD said, I will destroy man whom I have created from the face of the earth; both man, and beast, and the creeping thing, and the fowls of the air; for it repenteth me that I have made them.

But Noah found grace in the eyes of the LORD.

Noah Builds the Ark
Genesis 6:13, 14, 19, 22

And God said unto Noah, The end of all flesh is come before me; for the earth is filled with violence through them; and, behold, I will destroy them with the earth.

Make thee an ark of gopher wood; rooms shalt thou make in the ark, and shalt pitch it within and without with pitch.

And of every living thing of all flesh, two of every *sort* shalt thou bring into the ark, to keep *them* alive with thee; they shall be male and female.

Thus did Noah; according to all that God commanded him, so did he.

The Flood Comes
Genesis 7:7–9, 17–19

And Noah went in, and his sons, and his wife, and his sons' wives with him, into the ark, because of the waters of the flood.

Of clean beasts, and of beasts that *are* not clean, and of fowls, and of every thing that creepeth upon the earth,

There went in two and two unto Noah into the ark, the male and the female, as God had commanded Noah.

And the flood was forty days upon the earth; and the waters increased, and bare up the ark, and it was lift up above the earth.

And the waters prevailed, and were increased greatly upon the earth; and the ark went upon the face of the waters.

And the waters prevailed exceedingly upon the earth; and all the high hills, that *were* under the whole heaven, were covered.

Noah Leaves the Ark
Genesis 8:15–17, 20a

And God spake unto Noah, saying,

Go forth of the ark, thou, and thy wife, and thy sons, and thy sons' wives with thee.

Bring forth with thee every living thing that *is* with thee, of all flesh, *both* of fowl, and of cattle, and of every creeping thing that creepeth upon the earth; that they may breed abundantly in the earth, and be fruitful, and multiply upon the earth.

And Noah builded an altar unto the Lord.

God Promises the Rainbow
Genesis 9:12–15

And God said, This *is* the token of the covenant which I make between me and you and every living creature that *is* with you, for perpetual generations:

I do set my bow in the cloud, and it shall be for a token of a covenant between me and the earth.

And it shall come to pass, when I bring a cloud over the earth, that the bow shall be seen in the cloud:

And I will remember my covenant, which *is* between me and you and every living creature of all flesh; and the waters shall no more become a flood to destroy all flesh.

GOD CALLS ABRAM

God Sends Abram to a New Land
Genesis 12:1–4

Now the LORD had said unto Abram, Get thee out of thy country, and from thy kindred, and from thy father's house, unto a land that I will shew thee:

And I will make of thee a great nation, and I will bless thee, and make thy name great; and thou shalt be a blessing:

And I will bless them that bless thee, and curse him that curseth thee: and in thee shall all families of the earth be blessed.

So Abram departed, as the LORD had spoken unto him; and Lot went with him: and Abram *was* seventy and five years old when he departed out of Haran.

God Gives Abraham a Son
Genesis 18:10b, 11a, 12–14; 21:1–3

And, lo, Sarah thy wife shall have a son. And Sarah heard *it* in the tent door, which *was* behind him.

Now Abraham and Sarah *were* old *and* well stricken in age;

Therefore Sarah laughed within herself, saying, After I am waxed old shall I have pleasure, my lord being old also?

And the LORD said unto Abraham, Wherefore did Sarah laugh, saying, Shall I of a surety bear a child, which am old?

Is any thing too hard for the LORD? At the time appointed I will return unto thee, according to the time of life, and Sarah shall have a son.

And the LORD visited Sarah as he had said, and the LORD did unto Sarah as he had spoken.

For Sarah conceived, and bare Abraham a son in his old age, at the set time of which God had spoken to him.

And Abraham called the name of his son that was born unto him, whom Sarah bare to him, Isaac.

*A*nd God said, Let the earth bring
forth grass, the herb yielding seed,
and the fruit tree yielding fruit after
his kind . . . and it was so.

Genesis 1:11

*A*nd God saw every thing that he had made, and, behold, it was very good.

Genesis 1:31

God Gives Abraham a Test

And it came to pass after these things, that God did tempt Abraham, and said unto him, Abraham: and he said, Behold, *here* I *am.*

And he said, Take now thy son, thine only son Isaac, whom thou lovest, and get thee into the land of Mo-ri´-ah; and offer him there for a burnt offering upon one of the mountains which I will tell thee of.

And Abraham rose up early in the morning, and saddled his ass, and took two of his young men with him, and Isaac his son, and clave the wood for the burnt offering, and rose up, and went unto the place of which God had told him.

And Isaac spake unto Abraham his father, and said, My father: and he said, Here *am* I, my son. And he said, Behold the fire and the wood: but where *is* the lamb for a burnt offering?

And Abraham said, My son, God will provide himself a lamb for a burnt offering: so they went both of them together.

And they came to the place which God had told him of; and Abraham built an altar there, and laid the wood in order, and bound Isaac his son, and laid him on the altar upon the wood.

And Abraham stretched forth his hand, and took the knife to slay his son.

And the angel of the LORD called unto him out of heaven, and said, Abraham, Abraham: and he said, Here *am* I.

And he said, Lay not thine hand upon the lad, neither do thou any thing unto him: for now I know that thou fearest God, seeing thou hast not withheld thy son, thine only *son* from me.

And Abraham lifted up his eyes, and looked, and behold behind *him* a ram caught in a thicket by his horns: and Abraham went and took the ram, and offered him up for a burnt offering in the stead of his son.

JACOB LEARNS the HARD WAY

Esau Sells the Birthright

Genesis 25:31–33

And Jacob said, Sell me this day thy birthright.

And Esau said, Behold, I *am* at the point to die: and what profit shall this birthright do to me?

And Jacob said, Swear to me this day; and he sware unto him: and he sold his birthright unto Jacob.

Jacob Deceives His Brother and Father

Genesis 27:1–4, 15–17, 21–23, 30, 32–34, 41–44

And it came to pass, that when Isaac was old, and his eyes were dim, so that he could not see, he called Esau his eldest son, and said unto him, My son: and he said unto him, Behold, *here am* I.

And he said, Behold now, I am old, I know not the day of my death:

Now therefore take, I pray thee, thy weapons, thy quiver and thy bow, and go out to the field, and take me *some* venison;

And make me savoury meat, such as I love, and bring *it* to me, that I may eat; that my soul may bless thee before I die.

And Rebekah took goodly raiment of her eldest son Esau, which *were* with her in the house, and put them upon Jacob her younger son:

And she put the skins of the kids of the goats upon his hands, and upon the smooth of his neck:

And she gave the savoury meat and the bread, which she had prepared, into the hand of her son Jacob.

And Isaac said unto Jacob, Come near, I pray thee, that I may feel thee, my son, whether thou *be* my very son Esau or not.

And Jacob went near unto Isaac his father; and he felt him, and said, The voice *is* Jacob's voice, but the hands *are* the hands of Esau.

And he discerned him not, because his hands were hairy, as his brother Esau's hands: so he blessed him.

And it came to pass, as soon as Isaac had made an end of blessing Jacob, and Jacob was yet scarce gone out from the presence of Isaac his father, that Esau his brother came in from his hunting.

And Isaac his father said unto him, Who *art* thou? And he said, I *am* thy son, thy first-born Esau.

And Isaac trembled very exceedingly, and said, Who? where *is* he that hath taken venison, and brought *it* me, and I have eaten of all before thou camest, and have blessed him? yea, *and* he shall be blessed.

And when Esau heard the words of his father, he cried with a great and exceeding bitter cry, and said unto his father, Bless me, *even* me also, O my father.

And Esau hated Jacob because of the blessing wherewith his father blessed him: and Esau said in his heart, The days of mourning for my father are at hand; then will I slay my brother Jacob.

And these words of Esau her elder son were told to Rebekah: and she sent and called Jacob her younger son, and said unto him, Behold, thy brother Esau, as touching thee, doth comfort himself, *purposing* to kill thee.

Now therefore, my son, obey my voice; and arise, flee thou to Laban my brother to Haran;

And tarry with him a few days, until thy brother's fury turn away.

Jacob Comes Back
Genesis 31:3, 33:4

And the Lord said unto Jacob, Return unto the land of thy fathers, and to thy kindred; and I will be with thee.

And Esau ran to meet him, and embraced him, and fell on his neck, and kissed him: and they wept.

JOSEPH

Joseph Is with His Family
Genesis 37:3–5, 18–20

Now Israel loved Joseph more than all his children, because he *was* the son of his old age: and he made him a coat of *many* colours.

And when his brethren saw that their father loved him more than all his brethren, they hated him, and could not speak peaceably unto him.

And Joseph dreamed a dream, and he told *it* his brethren: and they hated him yet the more.

And when they saw him afar off, even before he came near unto them, they conspired against him to slay him.

And they said one to another, Behold, this dreamer cometh.

Come now therefore, and let us slay him, and cast him into some pit, and we will say, Some evil beast hath devoured him: and we shall see what will become of his dreams.

Joseph's Brothers Sell Him
Genesis 37:26–28

And Judah said unto his brethren, What profit *is it* if we slay our brother, and conceal his blood?

Come, and let us sell him to the Ish´-mee-lites, and let not our hand be upon him; for he *is* our brother *and* our flesh. And his brethren were content.

Then there passed by Midianites merchantmen; and they drew and lifted up Joseph out of the pit, and sold Joseph to the Ish´mee-lites for twenty *pieces* of silver: and they brought Joseph into Egypt.

Joseph Serves His Master
Genesis 39:1–6

And Joseph was brought down to Egypt; and Pot´-i-phar, an officer of Pharaoh, captain of the guard, an Egyptian, bought him of the hands of the Ish´-mee-lites, which had brought him down thither.

And the LORD was with Joseph, and he was a prosperous man; and he was in the house of his master the Egyptian.

And his master saw that the LORD *was* with him, and that the LORD made all that he did to prosper in his hand.

And Joseph found grace in his sight, and he served him: and he made him overseer over his house, and all *that* he had he put into his hand.

And it came to pass from the time *that* he had made him overseer in his house, and over all that he had, that the LORD blessed the Egyptian's house for Joseph's sake; and the blessing of the LORD was upon all that he had in the house, and in the field.

And he left all that he had in Joseph's hand; and he knew not aught he had, save the bread which he did eat. And Joseph was *a* goodly *person,* and well favoured.

The Master's Wife Tells a Lie
Genesis 39:17–20

And she spake unto him, according to these words, saying, The Hebrew servant, which thou hast brought unto us, came in unto me to mock me:

And it came to pass, as I lifted up my voice and cried, that he left his garment with me, and fled out.

And it came to pass, when his master heard the words of his wife, which she spake unto him, saying, After this manner did thy servant to me; that his wrath was kindled.

And Joseph's master took him, and put him into the prison, a place where the king's prisoners were bound: and he was there in the prison.

Joseph Helps the Keeper of the Prison
Genesis 39:21–23

But the LORD was with Joseph, and shewed him mercy, and gave him favour in the sight of the keeper of the prison.

And the keeper of the prison committed to Joseph's hand all the prisoners that *were* in the prison; and whatsoever they did there, he was the doer *of it.*

The keeper of the prison looked not to any thing *that was* under his hand; because the LORD was with him, and *that* which he did, the LORD made *it* to prosper.

Joseph Tells about the Dreams of the Butler and the Baker
Genesis 40:1–23

And it came to pass after these things, *that* the butler of the king of Egypt and *his* baker had offended their lord the king of Egypt.

And Pharaoh was wroth against two *of* his officers, against the chief of the butlers, and against the chief of the bakers.

And he put them in ward in the house of the captain of the guard, into the prison, the place where Joseph *was* bound.

And the captain of the guard charged Joseph with them, and he served them: and they continued a season in ward.

And they dreamed a dream both of them, each man his dream in one night, each man according to the interpretation of his dream, the butler and the baker of the king of Egypt, which *were* bound in the prison.

And Joseph came in unto them in the morning, and looked upon them, and, behold, they *were* sad.

And he asked Pharaoh's officers that *were* with him in the ward of his lord's house, saying, Wherefore look ye *so* sadly to-day?

And they said unto him, We have dreamed a dream, and *there is* no interpreter of it. And Joseph said unto them, *Do* not interpretations *belong* to God? tell me *them,* I pray you.

And the chief butler told his dream to Joseph, and said to him, In my dream, behold, a vine *was* before me;

And in the vine *were* three branches: and it *was* as though it budded, *and* her blossoms shot forth; and the clusters thereof brought forth ripe grapes:

I do set my bow in the cloud, and it shall be for a token of a covenant between me and the earth.

Genesis 9:13

*I*s any thing too hard for the LORD?
Genesis 18:14

And Pharaoh's cup *was* in my hand: and I took the grapes, and pressed them into Pharaoh's cup, and I gave the cup into Pharaoh's hand.

And Joseph said unto him, This *is* the interpretation of it: The three branches *are* three days:

Yet within three days shall Pharaoh lift up thine head, and restore thee unto thy place: and thou shalt deliver Pharaoh's cup into his hand, after the former manner when thou wast his butler.

But think on me when it shall be well with thee, and shew kindness, I pray thee, unto me, and make mention of me unto Pharaoh, and bring me out of this house:

For indeed I was stolen away out of the land of the Hebrews: and here also have I done nothing that they should put me into the dungeon.

When the chief baker saw that the interpretation was good, he said unto Joseph, I also *was* in my dream, and, behold, *I had* three white baskets on my head:

And in the uppermost basket *there was* all manner of bakemeats for Pharaoh; and the birds did eat them out of the basket upon my head.

And Joseph answered and said, This *is* the interpretation thereof: The three baskets *are* three days:

Yet within three days shall Pharaoh lift up thy head from off thee, and shall hang thee on a tree; and the birds shall eat thy flesh from off thee.

And it came to pass the third day, *which was* Pharaoh's birthday, that he made a feast unto all his servants: and he lifted up the head of the chief butler and of the chief baker among his servants.

And he restored the chief butler unto his butlership again; and he gave the cup into Pharaoh's hand:

But he hanged the chief baker: as Joseph had interpreted to them.

Yet did not the chief butler remember Joseph, but forgat him.

Joseph Helps Pharaoh
Genesis 41:1a, 14–16, 28b–30, 33–40

And it came to pass at the end of two full years, that Pharaoh dreamed:

Then Pharaoh sent and called Joseph, and they brought him hastily out of the dungeon:

and he shaved *himself,* and changed his raiment, and came in unto Pharaoh.

And Pharaoh said unto Joseph, I have dreamed a dream, and *there is* none that can interpret it: and I have heard say of thee, *that* thou canst understand a dream to interpret it.

And Joseph answered Pharaoh, saying, *It is* not in me: God shall give Pharaoh an answer of peace.

What God *is* about to do he sheweth unto Pharaoh.

Behold, there come seven years of great plenty throughout all the land of Egypt:

And there shall arise after them seven years of famine; and all the plenty shall be forgotten in the land of Egypt; and the famine shall consume the land;

Now therefore let Pharaoh look out a man discreet and wise, and set him over the land of Egypt.

Let Pharaoh do *this,* and let him appoint officers over the land, and take up the fifth part of the land of Egypt in the seven plenteous years.

And let them gather all the food of those good years that come, and lay up corn under the hand of Pharaoh, and let them keep food in the cities.

And that food shall be for store to the land against the seven years of famine, which shall be in the land of Egypt; that the land perish not through the famine.

And the thing was good in the eyes of Pharaoh, and in the eyes of all his servants.

And Pharaoh said unto his servants, Can we find *such a one* as this *is,* a man in whom the spirit of God *is?*

And Pharaoh said unto Joseph, Forasmuch as God hath shewed thee all this, *there is* none so discreet and wise as thou *art:*

Thou shalt be over my house, and according unto thy word shall all my people be ruled: only in the throne will I be greater than thou.

Joseph Is Kind to His Brothers

Genesis 42:1, 2; 43:13–16; 45:1–10

Now when Jacob saw that there was corn in Egypt, Jacob said unto his sons, Why do ye look one upon another?

And he said, Behold, I have heard that there is corn in Egypt: get you down thither, and buy for us from thence; that we may live, and not die.

Take also your brother, and arise, go again unto the man:

And God Almighty give you mercy before the man, that he may send away your other brother, and Benjamin. If I be bereaved *of my children,* I am bereaved.

And the men took that present, and they took double money in their hand, and Benjamin; and rose up, and went down to Egypt, and stood before Joseph.

And when Joseph saw Benjamin with them, he said to the ruler of his house, Bring *these* men home, and slay, and make ready; for *these* men shall dine with me at noon.

Then Joseph could not refrain himself before all them that stood by him; and he cried, Cause every man to go out from me. And there stood no man with him, while Joseph made himself known unto his brethren.

And he wept aloud: and the Egyptians and the house of Pharaoh heard.

And Joseph said unto his brethren, I *am* Joseph; doth my father yet live? And his brethren could not answer him; for they were troubled at his presence.

And Joseph said unto his brethren, Come near to me, I pray you. And they came near.

And he said, I *am* Joseph your brother, whom ye sold into Egypt.

Now therefore be not grieved, nor angry with yourselves, that ye sold me hither: for God did send me before you to preserve life.

For these two years *hath* the famine *been* in the land: and yet *there are* five years, in the which *there shall* neither *be* earing nor harvest.

And God sent me before you to preserve you a posterity in the earth, and to save your lives by a great deliverance.

So now *it was* not you *that* sent me hither, but God: and he hath made me a father to Pharaoh, and lord of all his house, and a ruler throughout all the land of Egypt.

Haste ye, and go up to my father, and say unto him, Thus saith thy son Joseph, God hath made me lord of all Egypt: come down unto me, tarry not:

And thou shalt dwell in the land of Goshen, and thou shalt be near unto me, thou, and thy children, and thy children's children, and thy flocks, and thy herds, and all that thou hast.

MOSES

The King Gives a Command
Exodus 1:22, 2:1–2

And Pharaoh charged all his people, saying, Every son that is born ye shall cast into the river, and every daughter ye shall save alive.

And there went a man of the house of Levi, and took *to wife* a daughter of Levi.

And the woman conceived, and bare a son: and when she saw him that he *was a* goodly *child,* she hid him three months.

Moses Is in the Bulrushes
Exodus 2:3

And when she could not longer hide him, she took for him an ark of bulrushes, and daubed it with slime and with pitch, and put the child therein; and she laid *it* in the flags by the river's brink.

Miriam Watches Moses
Exodus 2:4

And his sister stood afar off, to wit what would be done to him.

The Princess Finds Moses

Exodus 2:5–10

And the daughter of Pharaoh came down to wash *herself* at the river; and her maidens walked along by the river's side; and when she saw the ark among the flags, she sent her maid to fetch it.

And when she had opened *it,* she saw the child: and, behold, the babe wept. And she had compassion on him, and said, This *is one* of the Hebrews' children.

Then said his sister to Pharaoh's daughter, Shall I go and call to thee a nurse of the Hebrew women, that she may nurse the child for thee?

And Pharaoh's daughter said to her, Go. And the maid went and called the child's mother.

And Pharaoh's daughter said unto her, Take this child away, and nurse it for me, and I will give *thee* thy wages. And the woman took the child, and nursed it.

And the child grew, and she brought him unto Pharaoh's daughter, and he became her son. And she called his name Moses: and she said, Because I drew him out of the water.

God Calls Moses
Exodus 3:2–5, 9–12

And the angel of the LORD appeared unto him in a flame of fire out of the midst of a bush: and he looked, and, behold, the bush burned with fire, and the bush *was* not consumed.

And Moses said, I will now turn aside, and see this great sight, why the bush is not burnt.

And when the LORD saw that he turned aside to see, God called unto him out of the midst of the bush, and said, Moses, Moses. And he said, Here *am* I.

And he said, Draw not nigh hither: put off thy shoes from off thy feet, for the place whereon thou standest *is* holy ground.

Now therefore, behold, the cry of the children of Israel is come unto me: and I have also seen the oppression wherewith the Egyptians oppress them.

Come now therefore, and I will send thee unto Pharaoh, that thou mayest bring forth my people the children of Israel out of Egypt.

And Moses said unto God, Who *am* I, that I should go unto Pharaoh, and that I should bring forth the children of Israel out of Egypt?

And he said, Certainly I will be with thee; and this *shall* be a token unto thee, that I have sent thee: When thou hast brought forth the people out of Egypt, ye shall serve God upon this mountain.

God Leads Israel out of Egypt
Exodus 12:12, 13, 50, 51

For I will pass through the land of Egypt this night, and will smite all the firstborn in the land of Egypt, both man and beast; and against all the gods of Egypt I will execute judgment: I *am* the LORD.

And the blood shall be to you for a token upon the houses where ye *are:* and when I see the blood, I will pass over you, and the plague shall not be upon you to destroy *you,* when I smite the land of Egypt.

Thus did all the children of Israel; as the LORD commanded Moses and Aaron, so did they.

And it came to pass the self-same day, *that* the LORD did bring the children of Israel out of the land of Egypt by their armies.

God Protects the Israelites

Exodus 14:13–18, 21–23, 27–30

And Moses said unto the people, Fear ye not, stand still, and see the salvation of the LORD, which he will shew to you to-day: for the Egyptians whom ye have seen to-day, ye shall see them again no more for ever.

The LORD shall fight for you, and ye shall hold your peace.

And the LORD said unto Moses, Wherefore criest thou unto me? speak unto the children of Israel, that they go forward:

But lift thou up thy rod, and stretch out thine hand over the sea, and divide it: and the children of Israel shall go on dry *ground* through the midst of the sea.

And I, behold, I will harden the hearts of the Egyptians, and they shall follow them: and I will get me honour upon Pharaoh, and upon all his host, upon his chariots, and upon his horsemen.

And the Egyptians shall know that I *am* the LORD, when I have gotten me honour upon Pharaoh, upon his chariots, and upon his horsemen.

And Moses stretched out his hand over the sea; and the LORD caused the sea to go *back* by a strong east wind all that night, and made the sea dry *land,* and the waters were divided.

45

And the children of Israel went into the midst of the sea upon the dry *ground:* and the waters *were* a wall unto them on their right hand, and on their left.

And the Egyptians pursued, and went in after them to the midst of the sea, *even* all Pharaoh's horses, his chariots, and his horsemen.

And Moses stretched forth his hand over the sea, and the sea returned to his strength when the morning appeared; and the Egyptians fled against it; and the LORD overthrew the Egyptians in the midst of the sea.

And the waters returned, and covered the chariots, and the horsemen, *and* all the host of Pharaoh that came into the sea after them; there remained not so much as one of them.

But the children of Israel walked upon dry *land* in the midst of the sea; and the waters *were* a wall unto them on their right hand, and on their left.

Thus the LORD saved Israel that day out of the hand of the Egyptians; and Israel saw the Egyptians dead upon the sea shore.

God Gives His Law
Exodus 24:3, 7

And Moses came and told the people all the words of the LORD, and all the judgments: and all the people answered with one voice, and said, All the words which the LORD hath said will we do.

And he took the book of the covenant, and read in the audience of the people: and they said, All that the LORD hath said will we do, and be obedient.

The People Grumble and Moses Makes a Serpent

Numbers 21:5–9; John 3:14, 15

And the people spake against God, and against Moses, Wherefore have ye brought us up out of Egypt to die in the wilderness? for *there is* no bread, neither *is there any* water; and our soul loatheth this light bread.

And the LORD sent fiery serpents among the people, and they bit the people; and much people of Israel died.

Therefore the people came to Moses, and said, We have sinned, for we have spoken against the LORD, and against thee; pray unto the LORD, that he take away the serpents from us. And Moses prayed for the people.

And the LORD said unto Moses, Make thee a fiery serpent, and set it upon a pole: and it shall come to pass, that every one that is bitten, when he looketh upon it, shall live.

And Moses made a serpent of brass, and put it upon a pole, and it came to pass, that if a serpent had bitten any man, when he beheld the serpent of brass, he lived.

And as Moses lifted up the serpent in the wilderness, even so must the Son of man be lifted up:

That whosoever believeth in him should not perish, but have eternal life.

O LORD our Lord, how excellent
is thy name in all the earth!
Psalm 8:9

Be strong and of a good courage;
be not afraid, neither be thou dismayed: for the LORD thy God is
with thee whithersoever thou goest.

Joshua 1:9

JOSHUA

God Makes Joshua the Leader
Joshua 1:1, 2, 8, 9

Now after the death of Moses the servant of the LORD it came to pass, that the LORD spake unto Joshua the son of Nun, Moses' minister, saying,

Moses my servant is dead; now therefore arise, go over this Jordan, thou, and all this people, unto the land which I do give to them, *even* to the children of Israel.

This book of the law shall not depart out of thy mouth; but thou shalt meditate therein day and night, that thou mayest observe to do according to all that is written therein: for then thou shalt make thy way prosperous, and then thou shalt have good success.

Have not I commanded thee? Be strong and of a good courage; be not afraid, neither be thou dismayed: for the LORD thy God *is* with thee whithersoever thou goest.

God Gives Joshua Orders
Joshua 6:2–5

And the LORD said unto Joshua, See, I have given into thine hand Jericho, and the king thereof, *and* the mighty men of valour.

And ye shall compass the city, all ye men of war, *and* go round about the city once. Thus shalt thou do six days.

And seven priests shall bear before the ark seven trumpets of rams' horns: and the seventh day ye shall compass the city seven times, and the priests shall blow with the trumpets.

And it shall come to pass, that when they make a long *blast* with the ram's horn, *and* when ye hear the sound of the trumpet, all the people shall shout with a great shout; and the wall of the city shall fall down flat, and the people shall ascend up every man straight before him.

God Helps Joshua Win

Joshua 6:6–10, 14–16, 20, 21

And Joshua the son of Nun called the priests, and said unto them, Take up the ark of the covenant, and let seven priests bear seven trumpets of rams' horns before the ark of the LORD.

And he said unto the people, Pass on, and compass the city, and let him that is armed pass on before the ark of the LORD.

And it came to pass, when Joshua had spoken unto the people, that the seven priests bearing the seven trumpets of rams' horns passed on before the LORD, and blew with the trumpets: and the ark of the covenant of the LORD followed them.

And the armed men went before the priests that blew with the trumpets, and the rereward came after the ark, *the priests* going on, and blowing with the trumpets.

And Joshua had commanded the people, saying, Ye shall not shout, nor make any noise with your voice, neither shall *any* word proceed out of your mouth, until the day I bid you shout; then shall ye shout.

And the second day they compassed the city once, and returned into the camp: so they did six days.

And it came to pass on the seventh day, that they rose early about the dawning of the day, and compassed the city after the same manner seven times: only on that day they compassed the city seven times.

And it came to pass at the seventh time, when the priests blew with the trumpets, Joshua said unto the people, Shout; for the LORD hath given you the city.

So the people shouted when *the priests* blew with the trumpets: and it came to pass, when the people heard the sound of the trumpet, and the people shouted with a great shout, that the wall fell down flat, so that the people went up into the city, every man straight before him, and they took the city.

And they utterly destroyed all that *was* in the city, both man and woman, young and old, and ox, and sheep, and ass, with the edge of the sword.

GIDEON

God's People Disobey
Judges 6:1, 2

And the children of Israel did evil in the sight of the LORD: and the LORD delivered them into the hand of Midian seven years.

And the hand of Midian prevailed against Israel: *and* because of the Midianites the children of Israel made them the dens which *are* in the mountains, and caves, and strong holds.

God Makes a Promise
Judges 6:11b, 12–16

Gideon threshed wheat by the winepress, to hide *it* from the Midianites.

And the angel of the LORD appeared unto him, and said unto him, The LORD *is* with thee, thou mighty man of valour.

And Gideon said unto him, Oh my Lord, if the LORD be with us, why then is all this befallen us? and where *be* all his miracles which our fathers told us of, saying, Did not the LORD bring us up from Egypt? but now the LORD hath forsaken us, and delivered us into the hands of the Midianites.

And the LORD looked upon him, and said, Go in this thy might, and thou shalt save Israel from the hand of the Midianites: have not I sent thee?

And he said unto him, Oh my Lord, wherewith shall I save Israel? behold, my family *is* poor in Ma-nas´-seh, and I *am* the least in my father's house.

And the LORD said unto him, Surely I will be with thee, and thou shalt smite the Midianites as one man.

God Chooses the Army

Judges 7:2–7, 16–21

And the LORD said unto Gideon, The people that *are* with thee *are* too many for me to give the Midianites into their hands, lest Israel vaunt themselves against me, saying, Mine own hand hath saved me.

Now therefore go to, proclaim in the ears of the people, saying, Whosoever *is* fearful and afraid, let him return and depart early from mount Gil´-e-ad. And there returned of the people twenty and two thousand; and there remained ten thousand.

And the LORD said unto Gideon, The people *are* yet *too* many; bring them down unto the water, and I will try them for thee there: and it shall be, *that* of whom I say unto thee, This shall go with thee, the same shall go with thee; and of whomsoever I say unto thee, This shall not go with thee, the same shall not go.

So he brought down the people unto the water: and the LORD said unto Gideon, Every one that lappeth of the water with his tongue, as a dog lappeth, him shalt thou set by himself; likewise every one that boweth down upon his knees to drink.

And the number of them that lapped, *putting* their hand to their mouth, were three hundred men: but all the rest of the people bowed down upon their knees to drink water.

And the LORD said unto Gideon, By the three hundred men that lapped will I save you, and deliver the Midianites into thine hand: and let all the *other* people go every man unto his place.

And he divided the three hundred men *into* three companies, and he put a trumpet in every man's hand, with empty pitchers, and lamps within the pitchers.

And he said unto them, Look on me, and do likewise: and, behold, when I come to the outside of the camp, it shall be *that,* as I do, so shall ye do.

When I blow with a trumpet, I and all that *are* with me, then blow ye the trumpets also on every side of all the camp, and say, *The sword* of the LORD, and of Gideon.

So Gideon, and the hundred men that *were* with him, came unto the outside of the camp in the beginning of the middle watch; and they had but newly set the watch: and they blew the trumpets, and brake the pitchers that *were* in their hands.

And the three companies blew the trumpets, and brake the pitchers, and held the lamps in their left hands, and the trumpets in their right hands to blow *withal:* and they cried, The sword of the LORD, and of Gideon.

And they stood every man in his place round about the camp: and all the host ran, and cried, and fled.

SAMSON

God Promises a Way of Deliverance Judges 13:1, 2, 6, 7, 24

And the children of Israel did evil again in the sight of the LORD; and the LORD delivered them into the hand of the Philistines forty years.

And there was a certain man of Zorah, of the family of the Danites, whose name *was* Ma-no´-ah; and his wife *was* barren, and bare not.

Then the woman came and told her husband, saying, A man of God came unto me, and his countenance *was* like the countenance of an angel of God, very terrible: but I asked him not whence he *was,* neither told he me his name:

But he said unto me, Behold, thou shalt conceive, and bear a son; and now drink no wine nor strong drink, neither eat any unclean *thing:* for the child shall be a Nazarite to God from the womb to the day of his death.

And the woman bare a son, and called his name Samson: and the child grew, and the LORD blessed him.

Samson Wants His Own Way
Judges 16:4–6, 16–21

And it came to pass afterward, that he loved a woman in the valley of Sorek, whose name *was* Delilah.

And the lords of the Philistines came up unto her, and said unto her, Entice him, and see wherein his great strength *lieth,* and by what *means* we may prevail against him, that we may bind him to afflict him: and we will give thee every one of us eleven hundred *pieces* of silver.

And Delilah said to Samson, Tell me, I pray thee, wherein thy great strength lieth, and wherewith thou mightest be bound to afflict thee.

And it came to pass, when she pressed him

daily with her words, and urged him, *so* that his soul was vexed unto death;

That he told her all his heart, and said unto her, There hath not come a razor upon mine head; for I *have been* a Nazarite unto God from my mother's womb: if I be shaven, then my strength will go from me, and I shall become weak, and be like any *other* man.

And when Delilah saw that he had told her all his heart, she sent and called for the lords of the Philistines, saying, Come up this once, for he hath shewed me all his heart. Then the lords of the Philistines came up unto her, and brought money in their hand.

And she made him sleep upon her knees; and she called for a man, and she caused him to shave off the seven locks of his head; and she began to afflict him, and his strength went from him.

And she said, The Philistines *be* upon thee, Samson. And he awoke out of his sleep, and said, I will go out as at other times before, and shake myself. And he wist not that the LORD was departed from him.

But the Philistines took him, and put out his eyes, and brought him down to Gaza, and bound him with fetters of brass; and he did grind in the prison house.

Samson Goes God's Way

And it came to pass, when their hearts were merry, that they said, Call for Samson, that he may make us sport. And they called for Samson out of the prison house; and he made them sport: and they set him between the pillars.

And Samson said unto the lad that held him by the hand, Suffer me that I may feel the pillars whereupon the house standeth, that I may lean upon them.

Now the house was full of men and women; and all the lords of the Philistines *were* there; and *there were* upon the roof about three thousand men and women, that beheld while Samson made sport.

And Samson called unto the LORD, and said, O Lord GOD, remember me, I pray thee, and strengthen me, I pray thee, only this once, O God, that I may be at once avenged of the Philistines for my two eyes.

And Samson took hold of the two middle pillars upon which the house stood, and on which it was borne up, of the one with his right hand, and of the other with his left.

And Samson said, Let me die with the Philistines. And he bowed himself with *all his* might; and the house fell upon the lords, and upon all the people that *were* therein. So the dead which he slew at his death were more than *they* which he slew in his life.

DAVID

God Calls David
1 Samuel 16:7, 10, 11, 13a

But the LORD said unto Samuel, Look not on his countenance, or on the height of his stature; because I have refused him: for *the LORD seeth* not as man seeth; for man looketh on the outward appearance, but the LORD looketh on the heart.

Again, Jesse made seven of his sons to pass before Samuel. And Samuel said unto Jesse, The LORD hath not chosen these.

And Samuel said unto Jesse, Are here all *thy* children? And he said, There remaineth yet the youngest, and, behold, he keepeth the sheep. And Samuel said unto Jesse, Send and fetch him: for we will not sit down till he come hither.

The heavens declare the glory of God; and the firmament sheweth his handywork.

Psalm 19:1

O LORD; teach
me thy paths.
Psalm 25:4

Then Samuel took the horn of oil, and
anointed him in the midst of his brethren: and
the spirit of the LORD came upon David from
that day forward.

David Decides to Fight the Giant *1 Samuel 17:4, 24, 32–46*

And there went out a champion out of the
camp of the Philistines, named Go-li´-ath, of
Gath, whose height *was* six cubits and a span.

And all the men of Israel, when they saw
the man, fled from him, and were sore afraid.

And David said to Saul, Let no man's heart
fail because of him; thy servant will go and
fight with this Philistine.

And Saul said to David, Thou art not able
to go against this Philistine to fight with him:
for thou *art but* a youth, and he a man of war
from his youth.

And David said unto Saul, Thy servant kept
his father's sheep, and there came a lion, and a
bear, and took a lamb out of the flock:

And I went out after him, and smote him,
and delivered *it* out of his mouth: and when he
arose against me, I caught *him* by his beard,
and smote him, and slew him.

Thy servant slew both the lion and the bear: and this uncircumcised Philistine shall be as one of them, seeing he hath defied the armies of the living God.

David said moreover, The LORD that delivered me out of the paw of the lion, and out of the paw of the bear, he will deliver me out of the hand of this Philistine. And Saul said unto David, Go, and the LORD be with thee.

And Saul armed David with his armour, and he put an helmet of brass upon his head; also he armed him with a coat of mail.

And David girded his sword upon his armour, and he assayed to go; for he had not proved *it*. And David said unto Saul, I cannot go with these; for I have not proved *them*. And David put them off him.

And he took his staff in his hand, and chose him five smooth stones out of the brook, and put them in a shepherd's bag which he had, even in a scrip; and his sling *was* in his hand: and he drew near to the Philistine.

And the Philistine came on and drew near unto David; and the man that bare the shield *went* before him.

And when the Philistine looked about, and saw David, he disdained him: for he was *but* a youth, and ruddy, and of a fair countenance.

And the Philistine said unto David, *Am* I a dog, that thou comest to me with staves? And the Philistine cursed David by his gods.

And the Philistine said to David, Come to me, and I will give thy flesh unto the fowls of the air, and to the beasts of the field.

Then said David to the Philistine, Thou comest to me with a sword, and with a spear, and with a shield: but I come to thee in the name of the LORD of hosts, the God of the armies of Israel, whom thou hast defied.

This day will the LORD deliver thee into mine hand; and I will smite thee, and take thine head from thee; and I will give the carcases of the host of the Philistines this day unto the fowls of the air, and to the wild beasts of the earth; that all the earth may know that there is a God in Israel.

THE PSALMS

God Is Maker of All
Psalm 8:3–9

When I consider thy heavens, the work of thy fingers, the moon and the stars, which thou hast ordained;

What is man, that thou art mindful of him? and the son of man, that thou visitest him?

For thou hast made him a little lower than the angels, and hast crowned him with glory and honour.

Thou madest him to have dominion over the works of thy hands: thou hast put all *things* under his feet:

All sheep and oxen, yea, and the beasts of the field;

The fowl of the air, and the fish of the sea, *and whatsoever* passeth through the paths of the seas.

O LORD our Lord, how excellent *is* thy name in all the earth!

LORD, who shall abide in thy tabernacle? who shall dwell in thy holy hill?

He that walketh uprightly, and worketh righteousness, and speaketh the truth in his heart.

He that backbiteth not with his tongue, nor doeth evil to his neighbour, nor taketh up a reproach against his neighbour.

In whose eyes a vile person is contemned; but he honoureth them that fear the LORD. *He that* sweareth to *his own* hurt, and changeth not.

He that putteth not out his money to usury, nor taketh reward against the innocent. He that doeth these *things* shall never be moved.

God Created All Things
Psalm 19:1–8

The heavens declare the glory of God; and the firmament sheweth his handywork.

Day unto day uttereth speech, and night unto night sheweth knowledge.

There is no speech nor language, *where* their voice is not heard.

Their line is gone out through all the earth, and their words to the end of the world. In them hath he set a tabernacle for the sun,

Which *is* as a bridegroom coming out of his chamber, *and* rejoiceth as a strong man to run a race.

His going forth *is* from the end of the heaven, and his circuit unto the ends of it: and there is nothing hid from the heat thereof.

The law of the LORD *is* perfect, converting the soul: the testimony of the LORD *is* sure, making wise the simple.

The statutes of the LORD *are* right, rejoicing the heart: the commandment of the LORD *is* pure, enlightening the eyes.

The fear of the LORD *is* clean, enduring for ever: the judgments of the LORD *are* true *and* righteous altogether.

72

God Is Merciful
Psalm 25:1–6

Unto thee, O LORD, do I lift up my soul.

O my God, I trust in thee: let me not be ashamed, let not mine enemies triumph over me.

Yea, let none that wait on thee be ashamed: let them be ashamed which transgress without cause.

Shew me thy ways, O LORD; teach me thy paths.

Lead me in thy truth, and teach me: for thou *art* the God of my salvation; on thee do I wait all the day.

Remember, O LORD, thy tender mercies and thy lovingkindnesses; for they *have been* ever of old.

God Is Powerful and Majestic
Psalm 29:1–5

Give unto the LORD, O ye mighty, give unto the LORD glory and strength.

Give unto the LORD the glory due unto his name; worship the LORD in the beauty of holiness.

The voice of the LORD *is* upon the waters: the God of glory thundereth: the LORD *is* upon many waters.

The voice of the LORD *is* powerful; the voice of the LORD *is* full of majesty.

The voice of the LORD breaketh the cedars; yea, the LORD breaketh the cedars of Lebanon.

God Wants Our Praise
Psalm 34:1–3

I will bless the LORD at all times: his praise *shall* continually *be* in my mouth.

My soul shall make her boast in the LORD: the humble shall hear *thereof,* and be glad.

O magnify the LORD with me, and let us exalt his name together.

God Wants Our Trust
Psalm 37:1–5

Fret not thyself because of evildoers, neither be thou envious against the workers of iniquity.

For they shall soon be cut down like the grass, and wither as the green herb.

Trust in the LORD, and do good; so shalt thou dwell in the land, and verily thou shalt be fed.

Delight thyself also in the LORD; and he shall give thee the desires of thine heart.

Commit thy way unto the LORD; trust also in him; and he shall bring *it* to pass.

God Is Our Refuge
Psalm 46:1–5

God *is* our refuge and strength, a very present help in trouble.

Therefore will not we fear, though the earth be removed, and though the mountains be carried into the midst of the sea;

Though the waters thereof roar *and* be troubled, *though* the mountains shake with the swelling thereof. Selah.

There is a river, the streams whereof shall make glad the city of God, the holy *place* of the tabernacles of the most High.

God *is* in the midst of her; she shall not be moved: God shall help her, *and that* right early.

God Loves Fellowship
Psalm 63:1–4

O God, thou *art* my God; early will I seek thee: my soul thirsteth for thee, my flesh longeth for thee in a dry and thirsty land, where no water is;

To see thy power and thy glory, so *as* I have seen thee in the sanctuary.

Because thy lovingkindness *is* better than life, my lips shall praise thee.

Thus will I bless thee while I live: I will lift up my hands in thy name.

God Is Our Protector
Psalm 71:1–5

In thee, O LORD, do I put my trust: let me never be put to confusion.

Deliver me in thy righteousness, and cause me to escape: incline thine ear unto me, and save me.

Be thou my strong habitation, whereunto I may continually resort: thou hast given commandment to save me; for thou *art* my rock and my fortress.

Deliver me, O my God, out of the hand of the wicked, out of the hand of the unrighteous and cruel man.

For thou *art* my hope, O Lord GOD: *thou art* my trust from my youth.

God Is Our Dwelling Place
Psalm 90:1–6

LORD, thou hast been our dwelling place in all generations.

Before the mountains were brought forth, or ever thou hadst formed the earth and the world, even from everlasting to everlasting, thou *art* God.

Thou turnest man to destruction; and sayest, Return, ye children of men.

For a thousand years in thy sight *are but* as yesterday when it is past, and *as* a watch in the night.

Thou carriest them away as with a flood; they are *as* a sleep: in the morning *they are* like grass *which* groweth up.

In the morning it flourisheth, and groweth up; in the evening it is cut down, and withereth.

God Shows Lovingkindness

It is a good *thing* to give thanks unto the LORD, and to sing praises unto thy name, O most High:

To shew forth thy lovingkindness in the morning, and thy faithfulness every night,

Upon an instrument of ten strings, and upon the psaltery; upon the harp with a solemn sound.

For thou, LORD, hast made me glad through thy work: I will triumph in the works of thy hands.

O LORD, how great are thy works! *and* thy thoughts are very deep.

God Reigns on High
Psalm 93:1–5

The LORD reigneth, he is clothed with majesty; the LORD is clothed with strength, *wherewith* he hath girded himself: the world also is stablished, that it cannot be moved.

Thy throne *is* established of old: thou *art* from everlasting.

The floods have lifted up, O LORD, the floods have lifted up their voice; the floods lift up their waves.

The LORD on high *is* mightier than the noise of many waters, *yea, than* the mighty waves of the sea.

Thy testimonies are very sure: holiness becometh thine house, O LORD, for ever.

God Shows His Benefits
Psalm 103:1–5

Bless the LORD, O my soul: and all that is within me, *bless* his holy name.

Bless the LORD, O my soul, and forget not all his benefits:

Who forgiveth all thine iniquities; who healeth all thy diseases;

Who redeemeth thy life from destruction; who crowneth thee with lovingkindness and tender mercies;

Who satisfieth thy mouth with good *things; so that* thy youth is renewed like the eagle's.

God Does Wonderful Works
Psalm 111:1–6

Praise ye the LORD. I will praise the LORD with *my* whole heart, in the assembly of the upright, and *in* the congregation.

The works of the LORD *are* great, sought out of all them that have pleasure therein.

His work *is* honourable and glorious: and his righteousness endureth for ever.

He hath made his wonderful works to be remembered: the LORD *is* gracious and full of compassion.

He hath given meat unto them that fear him: he will ever be mindful of his covenant.

He hath shewed his people the power of his works, that he may give them the heritage of the heathen.

God Delights in Obedience
Psalm 112:1–7

Praise ye the LORD. Blessed *is* the man *that* feareth the LORD, *that* delighteth greatly in his commandments.

His seed *shall be* mighty upon the earth: the generation of the upright shall be blessed.

*F*rom the rising of the sun unto the going down of the same the LORD's name is to be praised.

Psalm 113:3

My help cometh from the LORD, which made heaven and earth.
Psalm 121:2

Wealth and riches *shall be* in his house: and his righteousness endureth for ever.

Unto the upright there ariseth light in the darkness: *he is* gracious, and full of compassion, and righteous.

A good man sheweth favour, and lendeth: he will guide his affairs with discretion.

Surely he shall not be moved for ever: the righteous shall be in everlasting remembrance.

He shall not be afraid of evil tidings: his heart is fixed, trusting in the LORD.

God Is to Be Praised
Psalm 113:1–9

Praise ye the LORD. Praise, O ye servants of the LORD, praise the name of the LORD.

Blessed be the name of the LORD from this time forth and for evermore.

From the rising of the sun unto the going down of the same the LORD's name *is* to be praised.

The LORD *is* high above all nations, *and* his glory above the heavens.

Who *is* like unto the LORD our God, who dwelleth on high,

Who humbleth *himself* to behold *the things that are* in heaven, and in the earth!

He raiseth up the poor out of the dust, *and* lifteth the needy out of the dunghill;

That he may set *him* with princes, *even* with the princes of his people.

He maketh the barren woman to keep house, *and to be* a joyful mother of children. Praise ye the LORD.

God Listens to Our Prayers
Psalm 116:1–2

I love the LORD, because he hath heard my voice *and* my supplications.

Because he hath inclined his ear unto me, therefore will I call upon *him* as long as I live.

God's Truth Lasts
Psalm 117:1–2

O praise the LORD, all ye nations: praise him, all ye people.

For his merciful kindness is great toward us: and the truth of the LORD *endureth* for ever. Praise ye the LORD.

God Will Give Wisdom
Psalm 119:97–104

O how love I thy law! it *is* my meditation all the day.

Thou through thy commandments hast made me wiser than mine enemies: for they *are* ever with me.

I have more understanding than all my teachers: for thy testimonies *are* my meditation.

I understand more than the ancients, because I keep thy precepts.

I have refrained my feet from every evil way, that I might keep thy word.

I have not departed from thy judgments: for thou hast taught me.

How sweet are thy words unto my taste! *yea, sweeter* than honey to my mouth!

Through thy precepts I get understanding: therefore I hate every false way.

God Is Our Keeper
Psalm 121:1–8

I will lift up mine eyes unto the hills, from whence cometh my help.

My help *cometh* from the LORD, which made heaven and earth.

He will not suffer thy foot to be moved: he that keepeth thee will not slumber.

Behold, he that keepeth Israel shall neither slumber nor sleep.

The LORD *is* thy keeper: the LORD *is* thy shade upon thy right hand.

The sun shall not smite thee by day, nor the moon by night.

The LORD shall preserve thee from all evil: he shall preserve thy soul.

The LORD shall preserve thy going out and thy coming in from this time forth, and even for evermore.

DANIEL

The King Makes the Image
Daniel 3:1a, 4–6

Neb-u-chad-nez´-zar the king made an image of gold,

Then an herald cried aloud, To you it is commanded, O people, nations, and languages,

That at what time ye hear the sound of the cornet, flute, harp, sackbut, psaltery, dulcimer, and all kinds of music, ye fall down and worship the golden image that Neb-u-chad-nez´-zar the king hath set up:

And whoso falleth not down and worshippeth shall the same hour be cast into the midst of a burning fiery furnace.

God's Men Do Not Bow to the Image
Daniel 3:8, 12–18

Wherefore at that time certain Chal-de´-ans came near, and accused the Jews.

There are certain Jews whom thou hast set over the affairs of the province of Babylon, Sha´-drach, Me´-shach, and Abed-nego; these men, O king, have not regarded thee: they serve not thy gods, nor worship the golden image which thou hast set up.

Then Neb-u-chad-nez´-zar in *his* rage and fury commanded to bring Sha´-drach, Me´-shach, and Abed-nego. Then they brought these men before the king.

Neb-u-chad-nez´-zar spake and said unto them, *Is it* true, O Sha´-drach, Me´-shach, and Abed-nego, do not ye serve my gods, nor worship the golden image which I have set up?

Now if ye be ready that at what time ye hear the sound of the cornet, flute, harp, sackbut, psaltery, and dulcimer, and all kinds of music, ye fall down and worship the image which I have made; *well:* but if ye worship not, ye shall be cast the same hour into the midst of a burning fiery furnace; and who *is* that God that shall deliver you out of my hands?

Sha´-drach, Me´-shach, and Abed-nego, answered and said to the king, O Neb-u-chad-nez´-zar, we *are* not careful to answer thee in this matter.

If it be *so,* our God whom we serve is able to deliver us from the burning fiery furnace, and he will deliver *us* out of thine hand, O king.

But if not, be it known unto thee, O king, that we will not serve thy gods, nor worship the golden image which thou hast set up.

God Protects His Men
Daniel 3:19–29

Then was Neb-u-chad-nez´-zar full of fury, and the form of his visage was changed against Sha´-drach, Me´-shach, and Abed-nego: *therefore* he spake, and commanded that they should heat the furnace one seven times more than it was wont to be heated.

And he commanded the most mighty men that *were* in his army to bind Sha´-drach, Me´-shach, and Abed-nego, *and* to cast *them* into the burning fiery furnace.

Then these men were bound in their coats, their hosen, and their hats, and their *other* garments, and were cast into the midst of the burning fiery furnace.

Therefore because the king's commandment was urgent, and the furnace exceeding hot, the flame of the fire slew those men that took up Sha´-drach, Me´-shach, and Abed-nego.

And these three men, Sha´-drach, Me´-shach, and Abed-nego, fell down bound into the midst of the burning fiery furnace.

Then Neb-u-chad-nez´-zar the king was astonied, and rose up in haste, *and* spake, and said unto his counsellors, Did not we cast three men bound into the midst of the fire? They answered and said unto the king, True, O king.

He answered and said, Lo, I see four men loose, walking in the midst of the fire, and they have no hurt; and the form of the fourth is like the Son of God.

Then Neb-u-chad-nez´-zar came near to the mouth of the burning fiery furnace, *and* spake, and said, Sha´-drach, Me´-shach, and Abed-nego, ye servants of the most high God, come forth, and come *hither.* Then Shad´-rach, Me´-shach, and Abed-nego, came forth of the midst of the fire.

And the princes, governors, and captains, and the king's counsellors, being gathered together, saw these men, upon whose bodies the fire had no power, nor was an hair of their head singed, neither were their coats changed, nor the smell of fire had passed on them.

Then Neb-u-chad-nez´-zar spake, and said, Blessed *be* the God of Sha´-drach, Me´-shach, and Abed-nego, who hath sent his angel, and delivered his servants that trusted in him, and have changed the king's word, and yielded their bodies, that they might not serve nor worship any god, except their own God.

Therefore I make a decree, That every people, nation, and language, which speak any thing amiss against the God of Sha´-drach, Me´-shach, and Abed-nego, shall be cut in pieces, and their houses shall be made a dung-hill: because there is no other God that can deliver after this sort.

The King Honors Daniel
Daniel 6:3

Then this Daniel was preferred above the presidents and princes, because an excellent spirit *was* in him; and the king thought to set him over the whole realm.

The King Makes a Decree
Daniel 6:6–9

Then these presidents and princes assembled together to the king, and said thus unto him, King Da-ri´-us, live for ever.

All the presidents of the kingdom, the governors, and the princes, the counsellors, and the captains, have consulted together to establish a royal statute, and to make a firm decree that whosoever shall ask a petition of any God or man for thirty days, save of thee, O king, he shall be cast into the den of lions.

Now, O king, establish the decree, and sign the writing, that it be not changed, according to the law of the Medes and Persians, which altereth not.

Wherefore king Da-ri´-us signed the writing and the decree.

Daniel Obeys God
Daniel 6:10–19

Now when Daniel knew that the writing was signed, he went into his house; and his windows being open in his chamber toward

Jerusalem, he kneeled upon his knees three times a day, and prayed, and gave thanks before his God, as he did aforetime.

Then these men assembled, and found Daniel praying and making supplication before his God.

Then they came near, and spake before the king concerning the king's decree; Hast thou not signed a decree, that every man that shall ask *a petition* of any God or man within thirty days, save of thee, O king, shall be cast into the den of lions? The king answered and said, The thing is true, according to the law of the Medes and Persians, which altereth not.

Then answered they and said before the king, That Daniel, which *is* of the children of the captivity of Judah, regardeth not thee, O king, nor the decree that thou hast signed, but maketh his petition three times a day.

Then the king, when he heard *these* words, was sore displeased with himself, and set *his* heart on Daniel to deliver him: and he laboured till the going down of the sun to deliver him.

Then these men assembled unto the king, and said unto the king, Know, O king, that the law of the Medes and Persians *is*, That no decree nor statute which the king establisheth may be changed.

Then the king commanded, and they brought Daniel, and cast *him* into the den of lions. *Now* the king spake and said unto Daniel, Thy God whom thou servest continually, he will deliver thee.

And a stone was brought, and laid upon the mouth of the den; and the king sealed it with his own signet, and with the signet of his lords; that the purpose might not be changed concerning Daniel.

Then the king went to his palace, and passed the night fasting: neither were instruments of music brought before him: and his sleep went from him.

Then the king arose very early in the morning, and went in haste unto the den of lions.

God Protects Daniel
Daniel 6:20–23

And when he came to the den, he cried with a lamentable voice unto Daniel: *and* the king spake and said to Daniel, O Daniel, servant of the living God, is thy God, whom thou servest continually, able to deliver thee from the lions?

Then said Daniel unto the king, O king, live for ever.

My God hath sent his angel, and hath shut the lions' mouths, that they have not hurt me: forasmuch as before him innocency was found in me; and also before thee, O king, have I done no hurt.

Then was the king exceeding glad for him, and commanded that they should take Daniel up out of the den. So Daniel was taken up out of the den, and no manner of hurt was found upon him, because he believed in his God.

JONAH

Jonah Disobeys God
Jonah 1:1–7, 15, 16

Now the word of the LORD came unto Jonah the son of A-mit´-tai, saying,

Arise, go to Nin´-e-veh, that great city, and cry against it; for their wickedness is come up before me.

But Jonah rose up to flee unto Tar´-shish from the presence of the LORD, and went down to Joppa; and he found a ship going to Tarshish: so he paid the fare thereof, and went down into it, to go with them unto Tarshish from the presence of the LORD.

But the LORD sent out a great wind into the sea, and there was a mighty tempest in the sea, so that the ship was like to be broken.

Then the mariners were afraid, and cried every man unto his god, and cast forth the wares that *were* in the ship into the sea, to lighten *it* of them. But Jonah was gone down into the sides of the ship; and he lay, and was fast asleep.

So the shipmaster came to him, and said unto him, What meanest thou, O sleeper? arise, call upon thy God, if so be that God will think upon us, that we perish not.

And they said every one to his fellow, Come, and let us cast lots, that we may know for whose cause this evil *is* upon us. So they cast lots, and the lot fell upon Jonah.

So they took up Jonah, and cast him forth into the sea: and the sea ceased from her raging.

Then the men feared the LORD exceedingly, and offered a sacrifice unto the LORD, and made vows.

Jonah Is inside the Fish
Jonah 1:17; 2:1, 10

Now the LORD had prepared a great fish to swallow up Jonah. And Jonah was in the belly of the fish three days and three nights.

Then Jonah prayed unto the LORD his God out of the fish's belly,

And the LORD spake unto the fish, and it vomited out Jonah upon the dry *land.*

Jonah Obeys God
Jonah 3:1–3a, 5, 10

And the word of the LORD came unto Jonah the second time, saying,

Arise, go unto Nin´-e-veh, that great city, and preach unto it the preaching that I bid thee.

So Jonah arose, and went unto Nin´-e-veh, according to the word of the LORD.

So the people of Nin´-e-veh believed God, and proclaimed a fast, and put on sackcloth, from the greatest of them even to the least of them.

And God saw their works, that they turned from their evil way; and God repented of the evil, that he had said that he would do unto them; and he did *it* not.

The New Testament

CHRISTMAS

The Angel Visits Mary
Luke 1:26–35

And in the sixth month the angel Gabriel was sent from God unto a city of Galilee named Nazareth,

To a virgin espoused to a man whose name was Joseph, of the house of David; and the virgin's name *was* Mary.

And the angel came in unto her, and said, Hail, *thou that art* highly favoured, the Lord *is* with thee: blessed *art* thou among women.

And when she saw *him,* she was troubled at his saying, and cast in her mind what manner of salutation this should be.

And the angel said unto her, Fear not, Mary: for thou hast found favour with God.

And, behold, thou shalt conceive in thy womb, and bring forth a son, and shalt call his name JESUS.

He shall be great, and shall be called the Son of the Highest: and the Lord God shall give unto him the throne of his father David:

And he shall reign over the house of Jacob for ever; and of his kingdom there shall be no end.

Then said Mary unto the angel, How shall this be, seeing I know not a man?

And the angel answered and said unto her, The Holy Ghost shall come upon thee, and the power of the Highest shall overshadow thee: therefore also that holy thing which shall be born of thee shall be called the Son of God.

Mary Praises God
Luke 1:46–50

And Mary said, My soul doth magnify the Lord, And my spirit hath rejoiced in God my Saviour.

For he hath regarded the low estate of his handmaiden: for, behold, from henceforth all generations shall call me blessed.

For he that is mighty hath done to me great things; and holy *is* his name.

And his mercy *is* on them that fear him from generation to generation.

Jesus Is Born
Luke 2:1–7

And it came to pass in those days, that there went out a decree from Caesar Augustus, that all the world should be taxed.

(*And* this taxing was first made when Cy-re´-ni-us was governor of Syria.)

And all went to be taxed, every one into his own city.

And Joseph also went up from Galilee, out of the city of Nazareth, into Judaea, unto the city of David, which is called Bethlehem; (because he was of the house and lineage of David:)

To be taxed with Mary his espoused wife, being great with child.

And so it was, that, while they were there, the days were accomplished that she should be delivered.

And she brought forth her firstborn son, and wrapped him in swaddling clothes, and laid him in a manger; because there was no room for them in the inn.

The Angel Visits the Shepherds
Luke 2:8–14

And there were in the same country shepherds abiding in the field, keeping watch over their flock by night.

And, lo, the angel of the Lord came upon them, and the glory of the Lord shone round about them: and they were sore afraid.

And the angel said unto them, Fear not: for, behold, I bring you good tidings of great joy, which shall be to all people.

For unto you is born this day in the city of David a Saviour, which is Christ the Lord.

And this *shall be* a sign unto you; Ye shall find the babe wrapped in swaddling clothes, lying in a manger.

And suddenly there was with the angel a multitude of the heavenly host praising God, and saying,

Glory to God in the highest and on earth peace, good will toward men.

The Shepherds Come to See Jesus
Luke 2:15–18

And it came to pass, as the angels were gone away from them into heaven, the shepherds said one to another, Let us now go even unto Bethlehem, and see this thing which is come to pass, which the Lord hath made known unto us.

And they came with haste, and found Mary, and Joseph, and the babe lying in a manger.

And when they had seen *it,* they made known abroad the saying which was told them concerning this child.

And all they that heard *it* wondered at those things which were told them by the shepherds.

Jesus Goes to Jerusalem
Luke 2:41, 42

Now his parents went to Jerusalem every year at the feast of the passover.

And when he was twelve years old, they went up to Jerusalem after the custom of the feast.

Jesus Does His Father's Business
Luke 2:43–50

And when they had fulfilled the days, as they returned, the child Jesus tarried behind in Jerusalem; and Joseph and his mother knew not *of it*.

But they, supposing him to have been in the company, went a day's journey; and they sought him among *their* kinsfolk and acquaintance.

And when they found him not, they turned back again to Jerusalem, seeking him.

And it came to pass, that after three days they found him in the temple, sitting in the midst of the doctors, both hearing them, and asking them questions.

And all that heard him were astonished at his understanding and answers.

And when they saw him, they were amazed: and his mother said unto him, Son, why hast thou thus dealt with us? behold, thy father and I have sought thee sorrowing.

And he said unto them, How is it that ye sought me? wist ye not that I must be about my Father's business?

And they understood not the saying which he spake unto them.

Jesus Goes Home
Luke 2:51, 52

And he went down with them, and came to Nazareth, and was subject unto them: but his mother kept all these sayings in her heart.

And Jesus increased in wisdom and stature, and in favour with God and man.

JESUS IS THE WORD

Jesus Has Always Been
John 1:1, 2

In the beginning was the Word, and the Word was with God, and the Word was God. The same was in the beginning with God.

Jesus Made All Things
John 1:3

All things were made by him; and without him was not any thing made that was made.

Jesus Is the Light of the World

John 1:4, 5, 9–12

In him was life; and the life was the light of men.

And the light shineth in darkness; and the darkness comprehended it not.

That was the true Light, which lighteth every man that cometh into the world.

He was in the world, and the world was made by him, and the world knew him not.

He came unto his own, and his own received him not.

But as many as received him, to them gave he power to become the sons of God, *even* to them that believe on his name.

THE TEMPTATION OF JESUS

The Devil Tempts Jesus with Stones *Matthew 4:1–4*

Then was Jesus led up of the Spirit into the wilderness to be tempted of the devil.

And when he had fasted forty days and forty nights, he was afterward an hungered.

And when the tempter came to him, he said, If thou be the Son of God, command that these stones be made bread.

But he answered and said, It is written, Man shall not live by bread alone, but by every word that proceedeth out of the mouth of God.

The Devil Tempts Jesus in the Temple *Matthew 4:5–7*

Then the devil taketh him up into the holy city, and setteth him on a pinnacle of the temple,

And saith unto him, If thou be the Son of God, cast thyself down: for it is written, He shall give his angels charge concerning thee: and in *their* hands they shall bear thee up, lest at any time thou dash thy foot against a stone.

Jesus said unto him, It is written again, Thou shalt not tempt the Lord thy God.

The Devil Takes Jesus to a High Mountain *Matthew 4:8–11*

Again, the devil taketh him up into an exceeding high mountain, and sheweth him all the kingdoms of the world, and the glory of them;

And saith unto him, All these things will I give thee, if thou wilt fall down and worship me.

Then saith Jesus unto him, Get thee hence, Satan: for it is written, Thou shalt worship the Lord thy God, and him only shalt thou serve.

Then the devil leaveth him, and, behold, angels came and ministered unto him.

JESUS MINISTERS

Nicodemus Comes to Jesus
John 3:1–3

There was a man of the Pharisees, named Nicodemus, a ruler of the Jews:

The same came to Jesus by night, and said unto him, Rabbi, we know that thou art a teacher come from God: for no man can do these miracles that thou doest, except God be with him.

Jesus answered and said unto him, Verily, verily, I say unto thee, Except a man be born again, he cannot see the kingdom of God.

*A*ll things were made by him;
and without him was not any
thing made that was made.

John 1:3

*B*ut he answered and said, It is written, Man shall not live by bread alone, but by every word that proceedeth out of the mouth of God.

Matthew 4:4

Jesus Explains about Being Born Again *John 3:4-13*

Nicodemus saith unto him, How can a man be born when he is old? can he enter the second time into his mother's womb, and be born?

Jesus answered, Verily, verily, I say unto thee, Except a man be born of water and *of* the Spirit, he cannot enter into the kingdom of God.

That which is born of the flesh is flesh; and that which is born of the Spirit is spirit.

Marvel not that I said unto thee, Ye must be born again.

The wind bloweth where it listeth, and thou hearest the sound thereof, but canst not tell whence it cometh, and whither it goeth: so is every one that is born of the Spirit.

Nicodemus answered and said unto him, How can these things be?

Jesus answered and said unto him, Art thou a master of Israel, and knowest not these things?

Verily, verily, I say unto thee, We speak that we do know, and testify that we have seen; and ye receive not our witness.

If I have told you earthly things, and ye believe not, how shall ye believe, if I tell you of heavenly things?

And no man hath ascended up to heaven, but he that came down from heaven, *even* the Son of man which is in heaven.

Jesus Tells about God's Great Love *John 3:14–17*

And as Moses lifted up the serpent in the wilderness, even so must the Son of man be lifted up:

That whosoever believeth in him should not perish, but have eternal life.

For God so loved the world, that he gave his only begotten Son, that whosoever believeth in him should not perish, but have everlasting life.

For God sent not his Son into the world to condemn the world; but that the world through him might be saved.

Jesus Heals a Sick Man
Luke 5:12–15

And it came to pass, when he was in a certain city, behold a man full of leprosy: who seeing Jesus fell on *his* face, and besought him, saying, Lord, if thou wilt, thou canst make me clean.

And he put forth *his* hand, and touched him, saying, I will: be thou clean. And immediately the leprosy departed from him.

And he charged him to tell no man: but go, and shew thyself to the priest, and offer for thy cleansing, according as Moses commanded, for a testimony unto them.

But so much the more went there a fame abroad of him: and great multitudes came together to hear, and to be healed by him of their infirmities.

THE WOMAN AT THE WELL

Jesus Offers Living Water
John 4:7–14, 25, 26

There cometh a woman of Samaria to draw water: Jesus saith unto her, Give me to drink.

(For his disciples were gone away unto the city to buy meat.)

Then saith the woman of Samaria unto him, How is it that thou, being a Jew, askest drink of me, which am a woman of Samaria? for the Jews have no dealings with the Samaritans.

Jesus answered and said unto her, If thou knewest the gift of God, and who it is that saith to thee, Give me to drink; thou wouldest have asked of him, and he would have given thee living water.

The woman saith unto him, Sir, thou hast nothing to draw with, and the well is deep: from whence then hast thou that living water?

Art thou greater than our father Jacob, which gave us the well, and drank thereof himself, and his children, and his cattle?

Jesus answered and said unto her, Whosoever drinketh of this water shall thirst again:

But whosoever drinketh of the water that I shall give him shall never thirst; but the water that I shall give him shall be in him a well of water springing up into everlasting life.

The woman saith unto him, I know that Messias cometh, which is called Christ: when he is come, he will tell us all things.

Jesus saith unto her, I that speak unto thee am *he*.

The Woman Invites Others
John 4:28, 29

The woman then left her waterpot, and went her way into the city, and saith to the men,

Come, see a man, which told me all things that ever I did: is not this the Christ?

JESUS PREACHES A SERMON

Luke 6:20–28

And he lifted up his eyes on his disciples, and said, Blessed *be ye* poor: for yours is the kingdom of God.

Blessed *are ye* that hunger now: for ye shall be filled. Blessed *are ye* that weep now: for ye shall laugh.

Blessed are ye, when men shall hate you, and when they shall separate you *from their company,* and shall reproach *you,* and cast out your name as evil, for the Son of man's sake.

Rejoice ye in that day, and leap for joy: for, behold, your reward *is* great in heaven: for in the like manner did their fathers unto the prophets.

But woe unto you that are rich! for ye have received your consolation.

Woe unto you that are full! for ye shall hunger. Woe unto you that laugh now! for ye shall mourn and weep.

Woe unto you, when all men shall speak well of you! for so did their fathers to the false prophets.

But I say unto you which hear, Love your enemies, do good to them which hate you,

Bless them that curse you, and pray for them which despitefully use you.

JESUS HEALS A LITTLE GIRL

The Little Girl Dies
Luke 8:41, 42, 49b

And, behold, there came a man named Ja-i'-rus, and he was a ruler of the synagogue: and he fell down at Jesus' feet, and besought him that he would come into his house:

For he had one only daughter, about twelve years of age, and she lay a-dying. But as he went the people thronged him.

There cometh one from the ruler of the synagogue's *house,* saying to him, Thy daughter is dead; trouble not the Master.

Jesus Performs a Miracle
Luke 8:50–56

But when Jesus heard *it,* he answered him, saying, Fear not: believe only, and she shall be made whole.

And when he came into the house, he suffered no man to go in, save Peter, and James, and John, and the father and the mother of the maiden.

And all wept, and bewailed her: but he said, Weep not; she is not dead, but sleepeth,

And they laughed him to scorn, knowing that she was dead.

And he put them all out, and took her by the hand, and called, saying, Maid, arise.

And her spirit came again, and she arose straightway: and he commanded to give her meat.

And her parents were astonished: but he charged them that they should tell no man what was done.

JESUS FEEDS A HUNGRY CROWD

The People Come to See Jesus
Luke 9:10–13

And the apostles, when they were returned, told him all that they had done. And he took them, and went aside privately into a desert place belonging to the city called Beth-sa´-i-da.

And the people, when they knew *it,* followed him: and he received them, and spake unto them of the kingdom of God, and healed them that had need of healing.

And when the day began to wear away, then came the twelve, and said unto him, Send the multitude away, that they may go into the towns and country round about, and lodge, and get victuals: for we are here in a desert place.

But he said unto them, Give ye them to eat. And they said, We have no more but five loaves and two fishes; except we should go and buy meat for all this people.

Jesus Feeds the People
Luke 9:14-17

For they were about five thousand men. And he said to his disciples, Make them sit down by fifties in a company.

And they did so, and made them all sit down.

Then he took the five loaves and the two fishes, and looking up to heaven, he blessed them, and brake, and gave to the disciples to set before the multitude.

And they did eat, and were all filled: and there was taken up of fragments that remained to them twelve baskets.

JESUS AND THE BLIND MAN

The Blind Man Begs
Luke 18:35–39

And it came to pass, that as he was come nigh unto Jericho, a certain blind man sat by the way side begging:

And hearing the multitude pass by, he asked what it meant.

And they told him, that Jesus of Nazareth passeth by.

And he cried, saying, Jesus, *thou* son of David, have mercy on me.

And they which went before rebuked him, that he should hold his peace: but he cried so much the more, *Thou* son of David, have mercy on me.

Jesus Makes the Blind Man See

Luke 18:40–43

And Jesus stood, and commanded him to be brought unto him: and when he was come near, he asked him,

Saying, What wilt thou that I shall do unto thee? And he said, Lord, that I may receive my sight.

And Jesus said unto him, Receive thy sight: thy faith hath saved thee.

And immediately he received his sight, and followed him, glorifying God: and all the people, when they saw *it,* gave praise unto God.

JESUS CALMS THE SEA

The Sea Obeys
Matthew 8:23–27

And when he was entered into a ship, his disciples followed him.

And, behold, there arose a great tempest in the sea, insomuch that the ship was covered with the waves: but he was asleep.

And his disciples came to *him,* and awoke him, saying, Lord, save us: we perish.

And he saith unto them, Why are ye fearful, O ye of little faith? Then he arose, and rebuked the winds and the sea; and there was a great calm.

But the men marvelled, saying, What manner of man is this, that even the winds and the sea obey him!

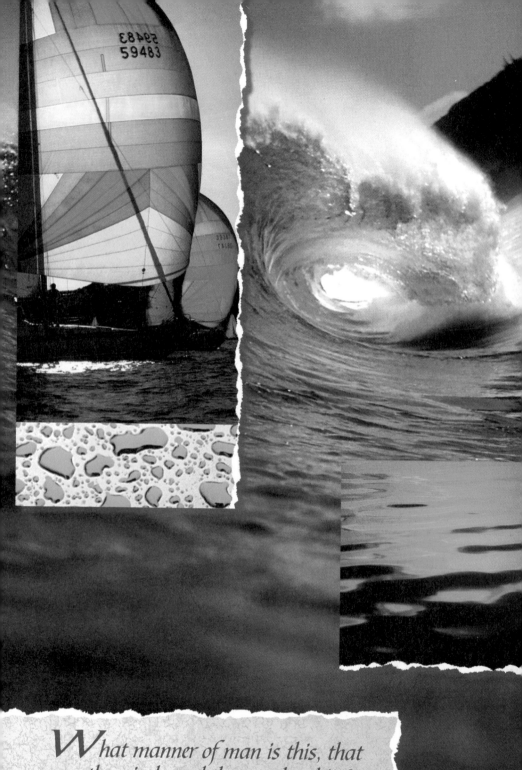

*W*hat manner of man is this, that even the winds and the sea obey him!

Matthew 8:27

*B*ut Jesus said, Suffer little
children, and forbid them not,
to come unto me: for of such
is the kingdom of heaven.
Matthew 19:14

JESUS WANTS CHILDREN TO COME TO HIM

Jesus Loves the Little Children
Matthew 19:13–15

Then were there brought unto him little children, that he should put *his* hands on them, and pray: and the disciples rebuked them.

But Jesus said, Suffer little children, and forbid them not, to come unto me: for of such is the kingdom of heaven.

And he laid *his* hands on them, and departed thence.

JESUS AND ZACCHAEUS

Zacchaeus Comes to See Jesus
Luke 19:1–5

And *Jesus* entered and passed through Jericho.

And, behold, *there was* a man named Zac-chae´-us, which was the chief among the publicans, and he was rich.

And he sought to see Jesus who he was; and could not for the press, because he was little of stature.

And he ran before, and climbed up into a sycomore tree to see him: for he was to pass that *way.*

And when Jesus came to the place, he looked up, and saw him, and said unto him, Zac-chae´-us, make haste, and come down; for to-day I must abide at thy house.

Jesus Goes to See Zacchaeus

Luke 19:6–10

And he made haste, and came down, and received him joyfully.

And when they saw it, they all murmured, saying, That he was gone to be guest with a man that is a sinner.

And Zac-chae´-us stood, and said unto the Lord; Behold, Lord, the half of my goods I give to the poor; and if I have taken any thing from any man by false accusation, I restore *him* fourfold.

And Jesus said unto him, This day is salvation come to this house, forsomuch as he also is a son of Abraham.

For the Son of man is come to seek and to save that which was lost.

EASTER

Jesus Is in the Upper Room
Luke 22:14–21

And when the hour was come, he sat down, and the twelve apostles with him.

And he said unto them, With desire I have desired to eat this passover with you before I suffer:

For I say unto you, I will not any more eat thereof, until it be fulfilled in the kingdom of God.

And he took the cup, and gave thanks, and said, Take this, and divide *it* among yourselves:

For I say unto you, I will not drink of the fruit of the vine, until the kingdom of God shall come.

And he took bread, and gave thanks, and brake *it,* and gave unto them, saying, This is my body which is given for you: this do in remembrance of me.

Likewise also the cup after supper, saying, This cup *is* the new testament in my blood, which is shed for you.

Jesus Is in the Garden
Luke 22:41–48

And he was withdrawn from them about a stone's cast, and kneeled down, and prayed,

Saying, Father, if thou be willing, remove this cup from me: nevertheless not my will, but thine, be done.

And there appeared an angel unto him from heaven, strengthening him.

And being in an agony he prayed more earnestly: and his sweat was as it were great drops of blood falling down to the ground.

And when he rose up from prayer, and was come to his disciples, he found them sleeping for sorrow,

And said unto them, Why sleep ye? rise and pray, lest ye enter into temptation.

And while he yet spake, behold a multitude, and he that was called Judas, one of the twelve, went before them, and drew near unto Jesus to kiss him.

But Jesus said unto him, Judas, betrayest thou the Son of man with a kiss?

Peter Denies Jesus
Luke 22:55–62

And when they had kindled a fire in the midst of the hall, and were set down together, Peter sat down among them.

But a certain maid beheld him as he sat by the fire, and earnestly looked upon him, and said, This man was also with him.

And he denied him, saying, Woman, I know him not.

And after a little while another saw him, and said, Thou art also of them. And Peter said, Man, I am not.

And about the space of one hour after another confidently affirmed, saying, Of a truth this *fellow* also was with him: for he is a Galilaean.

And Peter said, Man, I know not what thou sayest. And immediately, while he yet spake, the cock crew.

And the Lord turned, and looked upon Peter. And Peter remembered the word of the Lord, how he had said unto him, Before the cock crow, thou shalt deny me thrice.

And Peter went out, and wept bitterly.

Jesus Is before Pilate and Herod
Luke 23:1–5, 7, 11, 13, 14, 16, 18, 19, 25

And the whole multitude of them arose, and led him unto Pilate.

And they began to accuse him, saying, We found this *fellow* perverting the nation, and forbidding to give tribute to Caesar, saying that he himself is Christ a King.

And Pilate asked him, saying, Art thou the King of the Jews? And he answered him and said, Thou sayest *it*.

Then said Pilate to the chief priests and *to* the people, I find no fault in this man.

And they were the more fierce, saying, He stirreth up the people, teaching throughout all Jewry, beginning from Galilee to this place.

And as soon as he knew that he belonged unto Herod's jurisdiction, he sent him to Herod, who himself also was at Jerusalem at that time.

And Herod with his men of war set him at nought, and mocked *him,* and arrayed him in a gorgeous robe, and sent him again to Pilate.

And Pilate, when he had called together the chief priests and the rulers and the people,

Said unto them, Ye have brought this man unto me, as one that perverteth the people: and, behold, I, having examined *him* before you, have found no fault in this man touching those things whereof ye accuse him:

I will therefore chastise him, and release *him.*

And they cried out all at once, saying, Away with this *man,* and release unto us Barabbas:

(Who for a certain sedition made in the city, and for murder, was cast into prison.)

And he released unto them him that for sedition and murder was cast into prison, whom they had desired; but he delivered Jesus to their will.

Jesus Is on the Cross
Luke 23:32–46

And there were also two other, malefactors, led with him to be put to death.

And when they were come to the place, which is called Calvary, there they crucified him, and the malefactors, one on the right hand, and the other on the left.

Then said Jesus, Father, forgive them; for they know not what they do. And they parted his raiment, and cast lots.

And the people stood beholding. And the rulers also with them derided *him,* saying, He saved others; let him save himself, if he be Christ, the chosen of God.

And the soldiers also mocked him, coming to him, and offering him vinegar.

And saying, If thou be the king of the Jews, save thyself.

And a superscription also was written over him in letters of Greek, and Latin, and Hebrew, THIS IS THE KING OF THE JEWS.

And one of the malefactors which were hanged railed on him, saying, If thou be Christ, save thyself and us.

But the other answering rebuked him, saying, Dost not thou fear God, seeing thou art in the same condemnation?

And we indeed justly; for we receive the due reward of our deeds: but this man hath done nothing amiss.

And he said unto Jesus, Lord, remember me when thou comest into thy kingdom.

And Jesus said unto him, Verily I say unto thee, To-day shalt thou be with me in paradise.

And it was about the sixth hour, and there was a darkness over all the earth until the ninth hour.

And the sun was darkened, and the veil of the temple was rent in the midst.

And when Jesus had cried with a loud voice, he said, Father, into thy hands I commend my spirit: and having said thus, he gave up the ghost.

Jesus Rises from the Dead
Luke 24:1–9

Now upon the first *day* of the week, very early in the morning, they came unto the sepulchre, bringing the spices which they had prepared, and certain *others* with them.

And they found the stone rolled away from the sepulchre.

And they entered in, and found not the body of the Lord Jesus.

And it came to pass, as they were much perplexed thereabout, behold, two men stood by them in shining garments:

And as they were afraid, and bowed down *their* faces to the earth, they said unto them, Why seek ye the living among the dead?

He is not here, but is risen: remember how he spake unto you when he was yet in Galilee,

Saying, The Son of man must be delivered into the hands of sinful men, and be crucified, and the third day rise again.

And they remembered his words,

And returned from the sepulchre, and told all these things unto the eleven, and to all the rest.

Jesus Returns to Heaven
Acts 1:8–11

But ye shall receive power, after that the Holy Ghost is come upon you: and ye shall be witnesses unto me both in Jerusalem, and in all Judaea, and in Samaria, and unto the uttermost part of the earth.

And when he had spoken these things, while they beheld, he was taken up; and a cloud received him out of their sight.

And while they looked stedfastly toward heaven as he went up, behold, two men stood by them in white apparel;

Which also said, Ye men of Galilee, why stand ye gazing up into heaven? this same Jesus, which is taken up from you into heaven, shall so come in like manner as ye have seen him go into heaven.

PAUL

Saul Is at Stephen's Death
Acts 6:8, 10, 12–15; 7:55–60

And Stephen, full of faith and power, did great wonders and miracles among the people.

And they were not able to resist the wisdom and the spirit by which he spake.

And they stirred up the people, and the elders, and the scribes, and came upon *him,* and caught him, and brought *him* to the council,

And set up false witnesses, which said, This man ceaseth not to speak blasphemous words against this holy place, and the law:

For we have heard him say, that this Jesus of Nazareth shall destroy this place, and shall change the customs which Moses delivered us.

And all that sat in the council, looking stedfastly on him, saw his face as it had been the face of an angel.

But he, being full of the Holy Ghost, looked up stedfastly into heaven, and saw the glory of God, and Jesus standing on the right hand of God,

And said, Behold, I see the heavens opened, and the Son of man standing on the right hand of God.

Then they cried out with a loud voice, and stopped their ears, and ran upon him with one accord,

And cast *him* out of the city, and stoned *him:* and the witnesses laid down their clothes at a young man's feet, whose name was Saul.

And they stoned Stephen, calling upon *God,* and saying, Lord Jesus, receive my spirit.

And he kneeled down, and cried with a loud voice, Lord, lay not this sin to their charge. And when he had said this, he fell asleep.

Saul Hates the Christians
Acts 8:1–3

And Saul was consenting unto his death. And at that time there was a great persecution against the church which was at Jerusalem; and they were all scattered abroad throughout the regions of Judaea and Samaria, except the apostles.

And devout men carried Stephen *to his burial* and made great lamentation over him.

As for Saul, he made havoc of the church, entering into every house, and haling men and women committed *them* to prison.

Saul Becomes a Christian
Acts 9:3–9, 17, 18; 13:19

And as he journeyed, he came near Damascus: and suddenly there shined round about him a light from heaven:

And he fell to the earth, and heard a voice saying unto him, Saul, Saul, why persecutest thou me?

And he said, Who art thou, Lord? And the Lord said, I am Jesus whom thou persecutest: *it is* hard for thee to kick against the pricks.

And he trembling and astonished said, Lord, what wilt thou have me to do? And the Lord *said* unto him, Arise, and go into the city, and it shall be told thee what thou must do.

And the men which journeyed with him stood speechless, hearing a voice, but seeing no man.

And Saul arose from the earth; and when his eyes were opened, he saw no man: but they led him by the hand, and brought *him* into Damascus.

And he was three days without sight, and neither did eat nor drink.

And An-a-ni´-as went his way, and entered into the house; and putting his hands on him said, Brother Saul, the Lord, *even* Jesus, that appeared unto thee in the way as thou camest, hath sent me, that thou mightest receive thy sight, and be filled with the Holy Ghost.

And immediately there fell from his eyes as it had been scales: and he received sight forthwith, and arose, and was baptized.

Paul and Silas Are in Jail

Acts 16:22–32

And the multitude rose up together against them: and the magistrates rent off their clothes, and commanded to beat *them*.

And when they had laid many stripes upon them, they cast *them* into prison, charging the jailer to keep them safely:

Who, having received such a charge, thrust them into the inner prison, and made their feet fast in the stocks.

And at midnight Paul and Silas prayed, and sang praises unto God: and the prisoners heard them.

And suddenly there was a great earthquake, so that the foundations of the prison were shaken: and immediately all the doors were opened, and every one's bands were loosed.

And the keeper of the prison awaking out of his sleep, and seeing the prison doors open, he drew out his sword, and would have killed himself, supposing that the prisoners had been fled.

But Paul cried with a loud voice, saying, Do thyself no harm: for we are all here.

Then he called for a light, and sprang in, and came trembling, and fell down before Paul and Silas,

And brought them out, and said, Sirs, what must I do to be saved?

And they said, Believe on the Lord Jesus Christ, and thou shalt be saved, and thy house.

And they spake unto him the word of the Lord, and to all that were in his house.

Verses to Help in Our Daily Lives

THE BIBLE

God Wrote the Bible

Knowing this first, that no prophecy of the scripture is of any private interpretation.

For the prophecy came not in old time by the will of man: but holy men of God spake *as they were* moved by the Holy Ghost. *2 Peter 1:20, 21*

God's Word Brings Us Salvation and Instruction

And that from a child thou hast known the holy scriptures, which are able to make thee wise unto salvation through faith which is in Christ Jesus.

All scripture *is* given by inspiration of God, and *is* profitable for doctrine, for reproof, for correction, for instruction in righteousness:

That the man of God may be perfect, throughly furnished unto all good works.

As newborn babes, desire the sincere milk of the word, that ye may grow thereby:

These things have I written unto you that believe on the name of the Son of God; that ye may know that ye have eternal life, and that ye may believe on the name of the Son of God. *2 Timothy 3:15–17, 1 Peter 2:2, 1 John 5:13*

God's Word Is Powerful

For the word of God *is* quick, and powerful, and sharper than any two-edged sword, piercing even to the dividing asunder of soul and spirit, and of the joints and marrow, and *is* a discerner of the thoughts and intents of the heart. *Hebrews 4:12*

Thy word is a lamp unto my feet, and a light unto my path.

Psalm 119:105

*B*e thankful
unto him,
and bless his
name.
Psalm 100:4

God's Word Shows Us the Right Way

Thy word *is* a lamp unto my feet, and a light unto my path.

The entrance of thy words giveth light; it giveth understanding unto the simple. *Psalm 119:105, 130*

God's Word Helps Us to Do Right

Blessed *are* they that keep his testimonies, *and that* seek him with the whole heart.

They also do no iniquity: they walk in his ways.

Thy word have I hid in mine heart, that I might not sin against thee.

Psalm 119:2, 3, 11

God's Word Will Last Forever

For ever, O LORD, thy word is settled in heaven.

The grass withereth, the flower fadeth: but the word of our God shall stand for ever.

Heaven and earth shall pass away, but my words shall not pass away.

Being born again, not of corruptible seed, but of incorruptible, by the word of God, which liveth and abideth for ever.

For all flesh *is* as grass, and all the glory of man as the flower of grass. The grass withereth, and the flower thereof falleth away:

But the word of the Lord endureth for ever. And this is the word which by the gospel is preached unto you. *Psalm 119:89, Isaiah 40:8, Matthew 24:35, 1 Peter 1:23–25*

We Should Love and Honor God's Word

And I will delight myself in thy commandments, which I have loved.

O how love I thy law! it *is* my meditation all the day.

Thy word *is* very pure: therefore thy servant loveth it.

Thy words were found, and I did eat them; and thy word was unto me the joy and rejoicing of mine heart: for I am called by thy name, O LORD God of hosts. *Psalm 119:47, 97, 140; Jeremiah 15:16*

HEAVEN

Heaven Is a Real Place

Let not your heart be troubled: ye believe in God, believe also in me.

In my Father's house are many mansions: if *it were* not *so,* I would have told you. I go to prepare a place for you.

And if I go and prepare a place for you, I will come again, and receive you unto myself; that where I am, *there* ye may be also.

And whither I go ye know, and the way ye know. *John 14:1–4*

Who May Go to Heaven

Thomas saith unto him, Lord, we know not whither thou goest; and how can we know the way?

Jesus saith unto him, I am the way, the truth, and the life: no man cometh unto the Father, but by me.

For God so loved the world, that he gave his only begotten Son, that whosoever believeth in him should not perish, but have everlasting life.

For God sent not his Son into the world to condemn the world; but that the world through him might be saved.

Behold, I stand at the door, and knock: if any man hear my voice, and open the door, I will come in to him, and will sup with him, and he with me. *John 14:5, 6; John 3:16, 17; Revelation 3:20*

Jesus Is Coming Again

But I would not have you to be ignorant, brethren, concerning them which are asleep, that ye sorrow not, even as others which have no hope.

For if we believe that Jesus died and rose again, even so them also which sleep in Jesus will God bring with him.

For this we say unto you by the word of the Lord, that we which are alive *and* remain unto the coming of the Lord shall not prevent them which are asleep.

For the Lord himself shall descend from heaven with a shout, with the voice of the archangel, and with the trump of God: and the dead in Christ shall rise first:

Then we which are alive *and* remain shall be caught up together with them in the clouds, to meet the Lord in the air: and so shall we ever be with the Lord.

Wherefore comfort one another with these words. *1 Thessalonians 4:13–18*

PRAYER

Pray with Sin Confessed

If I regard iniquity in my heart, the Lord will not hear *me*.   *Psalm 66:18*

Pray in Secret

But thou, when thou prayest, enter into thy closet, and when thou hast shut thy door, pray to thy Father which is in secret; and thy Father which seeth in secret shall reward thee openly.   *Matthew 6:6*

*P*ray with a Thankful Heart

Enter into his gates with thanksgiving, *and* into his courts with praise: be thankful unto him, *and* bless his name.

For the LORD *is* good; his mercy *is* everlasting; and his truth *endureth* to all generations. *Psalm 100:4, 5*

*P*ray about Everything

Be careful for nothing; but in every thing by prayer and supplication with thanksgiving let your requests be made known unto God. *Philippians 4:6*

*A*sk God for What You Need

Verily, verily, I say unto you, Whatsoever ye shall ask the Father in my name, he will give *it* you.

Hitherto have ye asked nothing in my name: ask, and ye shall receive, that your joy may be full.

And this is the confidence that we have in him, that, if we ask any thing according to his will, he heareth us:

And if we know that he hear us, whatsoever we ask, we know that we have the petitions that we desired of him. *John 16:23b, 24; 1 John 5:14, 15*

*B*elieve God Will Answer Your Prayer

But without faith *it is* impossible to please *him;* for he that cometh to God must believe that he is, and *that* he is a rewarder of them that diligently seek him. *Hebrews 11:6*

OUR TONGUE

Speak Wisely

In the lips of him that hath understanding
wisdom is found: but a rod *is* for the back of
him that is void of understanding.

Who *is* a wise man and endued with knowledge among you? let him shew out of a good
conversation his works with meekness of wisdom.
Proverbs 10:13, James 3:13

Speak Pleasantly

Pleasant words *are as* an honeycomb, sweet
to the soul, and health to the bones.

A word fitly spoken *is like* apples of gold in
pictures of silver.

For he that will love life, and see good days, let him refrain his tongue from evil, and his lips that they speak no guile. *Proverbs 16:24, 25:11; 1 Peter 3:10*

Speak Truthfully

The lip of truth shall be established for ever: but a lying tongue *is* but for a moment.

Thou shalt not bear false witness against thy neighbour. *Proverbs 12:19, Exodus 20:16*

Speak Good Things

Keep thy tongue from evil, and thy lips from speaking guile. *Psalm 34:13*

The Tongue Is Little but It Can Do Great Harm

For in many things we offend all. If any man offend not in word, the same *is* a perfect man, *and* able also to bridle the whole body.

Behold, we put bits in the horses' mouths, that they may obey us; and we turn about their whole body.

Behold also the ships, which though *they be* so great, and *are* driven of fierce winds, yet are they turned about with a very small helm, whithersoever the governor listeth.

Even so the tongue is a little member, and boasteth great things. Behold, how great a matter a little fire kindleth! *James 3:2–5*

ABOUT MOTHER AND FATHER

We Should Obey Them

Children, obey your parents in the Lord: for this is right.

Honour thy father and mother; which is the first commandment with promise;

That it may be well with thee, and thou mayest live long on the earth.

Children, obey *your* parents in all things: for this is well pleasing unto the Lord.

My son, hear the instruction of thy father, and forsake not the law of thy mother. *Ephesians 6:1–3; Exodus 20:12; Proverbs 1:8*

We Should Honor Them

Honour thy father and thy mother: that thy days may be long upon the land which the LORD thy God giveth thee.

For God commanded, saying, Honour thy father and mother: and, He that curseth father or mother, let him die the death.

Honour thy father and *thy* mother: and, Thou shalt love thy neighbor as thyself. *Exodus 20:12, Matthew 15:4, 19:19*

We Should Make Them Happy

A wise son maketh a glad father: but a foolish man despiseth his mother. *Proverbs 15:20*

My son, hear the instruction of thy father, and forsake not the law of thy mother.

Proverbs 1:8

*I*n all thy ways acknowledge him,
and he shall direct thy paths.

Proverbs 3:6

ABOUT LEARNING

God Wants Us to Be Wise

Happy *is* the man *that* findeth wisdom, and the man *that* getteth understanding.

For the merchandise of it *is* better than the merchandise of silver, and the gain thereof than fine gold.

For wisdom *is* better than rubies; and all the things that may be desired are not to be compared to it.

Then I saw that wisdom excelleth folly, as far as light excelleth darkness.

Wisdom strengtheneth the wise more than ten mighty *men* which are in the city.   *Proverbs 3:13, 14; 8:11; Ecclesiastes 2:13; 7:19*

How We Can Be Wise

And unto man he said, Behold, the fear of the Lord, that *is* wisdom; and to depart from evil *is* understanding.

If any of you lack wisdom, let him ask of God, that giveth to all *men* liberally, and upbraideth not; and it shall be given him.

But let him ask in faith, nothing wavering. For he that wavereth is like a wave of the sea driven with the wind and tossed.

Wisdom *is* the principal thing; *therefore* get wisdom: and with all thy getting get understanding. *Job 28:28; James 1:5, 6; Proverbs 4:7*

We Should Study to Please God

Study to shew thyself approved unto God, a workman that needeth not to be ashamed, rightly dividing the word of truth. *2 Timothy 2:15*

We Should Work Hard to Please God

And whatsoever ye do, do *it* heartily, as to the Lord, and not unto men;

Knowing that of the Lord ye shall receive the reward of the inheritance: for ye serve the Lord Christ. *Colossians 3:23, 24*

MEMORY WORK

ABC BIBLE VERSES

All have sinned, and come short of the glory of
God. —*Romans 3:23*

Believe on the Lord Jesus Christ, and thou shalt
be saved. —*Acts 16:31*

Children, obey your parents in the Lord: for this
is right. —*Ephesians 6:1*

Depart from evil, and do good. —*Psalm 34:14*

Even a child is known by his doings.
—*Proverbs 20:11*

Fear not: for I am with thee. —*Isaiah 43:5*

God is love. —*1 John 4:8*

Honour thy father and thy mother. —*Exodus 20:12*

If ye shall ask anything in my name, I will do it.
—*John 14:14*

Jesus saith unto him, I am the way, the truth,
and the life: no man cometh unto the
Father, but by me. —*John 14:6*

Keep thy tongue from evil. —*Psalm 34:13*

Look unto me, and be ye saved. —*Isaiah 45:22*

My son, give me thine heart. —*Proverbs 23:26*

No man can serve two masters. —*Matthew 6:24*

O give thanks unto the Lord; for he is good.
—*Psalm 118:1*

Praise ye the Lord: for it is good to sing praises
unto our God. —*Psalm 147:1*

Quit you like men, be strong.
—*1 Corinthians 16:13*

Remember the sabbath day, to keep it holy.
—*Exodus 20:8*

Seek ye the Lord while he may be found.
—*Isaiah 55:6*

Thou God seest me. —*Genesis 16:13*

Unto thee, O God, do we give thanks.
—*Psalm 75:1*

Verily, verily, I say unto you, Whatsoever ye shall
ask the Father in my name, he will give it
you. —*John 16:23*

What time I am afraid, I will trust in Thee.
—*Psalm 56:3*

Exceeding great and precious promises are given
unto us. —*2 Peter 1:4*

Ye are the light of the world. —*Matthew 5:14*

Zion heard, and was glad. —*Psalm 97:8*

Bible Memory Verses for the Books of the New Testament

Matthew 22:37. Jesus said unto him, Thou shalt love the Lord thy God with all thy heart, and with all thy soul, and with all thy mind.

Mark 10:14. Suffer the little children to come unto me, and forbid them not: for of such is the kingdom of God.

Luke 1:37. For with God nothing shall be impossible.

John 3:16. For God so loved the world, that he gave his only begotten Son, that whosoever believeth in him should not perish, but have everlasting life.

Acts 3:19a. Repent ye therefore, and be converted, that your sins may be blotted out.

Romans 8:31b. If God be for us, who can be against us?

1 Corinthians 13:13. And now abideth faith, hope, charity, these three; but the greatest of these is charity.

2 Corinthians 5:17. Therefore if any man be in Christ, *he is* a new creature: old things are passed away; behold, all things are become new.

Galatians 6:9. And let us not be weary in well doing: for in due season we shall reap, if we faint not.

Ephesians 2:8. For by grace are ye saved through faith; and that not of yourselves: *it is* the gift of God.

Philippians 4:4. Rejoice in the Lord alway: *and* again I say, Rejoice.

Colossians 3:23. And whatsoever ye do, do it heartily, as to the Lord, and not unto men.

1 Thessalonians 5:16. Rejoice evermore.

2 Thessalonians 3:3. But the Lord is faithful, who shall stablish you, and keep *you from evil.*

1 Timothy 6:6. But godliness with contentment is great gain.

2 Timothy 2:15. Study to shew thyself approved unto God, a workman that needeth not to be ashamed, rightly dividing the word of truth.

Titus 3:5a. Not by works of righteousness which we have done, but according to his mercy he saved us.

Philemon 3. Grace to you, and peace, from God our Father and the Lord Jesus Christ.

Hebrews 13:8. Jesus Christ the same yesterday, and to day, and for ever.

James 4:8a. Draw nigh to God, and he will draw nigh to you.

1 Peter 5:7. Casting all your care upon him; for he careth for you.

2 Peter 3:18a. But grow in grace, and *in* the knowledge of our Lord and Saviour Jesus Christ.

1 John 1:5b. God is light, and in him is no darkness at all.

2 John 6a. And this is love, that we walk after his commandments.

3 John 11a. Follow not that which is evil, but that which is good.

Jude 25. To the only wise God our Saviour, *be* glory and majesty, dominion and power, both now and ever.

Revelation 3:20. Behold, I stand at the door, and knock: if any man hear my voice, and open the door, I will come in to him, and will sup with him, and he with me.

THE LORD'S PRAYER

Matthew 6:9b-13

Our Father which art in heaven, Hallowed be thy name.

Thy kingdom come. Thy will be done in earth, as *it is* in heaven.

Give us this day our daily bread.

And forgive us our debts, as we forgive our debtors.

And lead us not into temptation, but deliver us from evil: For thine is the kingdom, and the power, and the glory, for ever. Amen.

THE TEN COMMANDMENTS

Exodus 20

Thou shalt have no other gods before me.

Thou shalt not make unto thee any graven image, or any likeness *of any thing* that *is* in heaven above, or that *is* in the earth beneath, or that *is* in the water under the earth:

Thou shalt not bow down thyself to them, nor serve them.

Thou shalt not take the name of the LORD thy God in vain; for the LORD will not hold him guiltless that taketh his name in vain.

Remember the sabbath day, to keep it holy.

Honour thy father and thy mother: that thy days may be long upon the land which the LORD thy God giveth thee.

Thou shalt not kill.

Thou shalt not commit adultery.

Thou shalt not steal.

Thou shalt not bear false witness against thy neighbour.

Thou shalt not covet thy neighbour's house nor any thing that *is* thy neighbour's.

*P*salm 100

Make a joyful noise unto the LORD, all ye lands. Serve the LORD with gladness: come before his presence with singing.

Know ye that the LORD he *is* God: *it is* he *that* hath made us, and not we ourselves; *we are* his people, and the sheep of his pasture.

Enter into his gates with thanksgiving, *and* into his courts with praise: be thankful unto him, *and* bless his name.

For the LORD *is* good; his mercy *is* everlasting: and his truth *endureth* to all generations.

Psalm 23

The LORD *is* my shepherd; I shall not want.

He maketh me to lie down in green pastures: he leadeth me beside the still waters.

He restoreth my soul: he leadeth me in the paths of righteousness for his name's sake.

Yea, though I walk through the valley of the shadow of death, I will fear no evil: for thou *art* with me; thy rod and thy staff they comfort me.

Thou preparest a table before me in the presence of mine enemies: thou anointest my head with oil; my cup runneth over.

Surely goodness and mercy shall follow me all the days of my life: and I will dwell in the house of the LORD for ever.

John 3:16-17

For God so loved the world, that he gave his only begotten Son, that whosoever believeth in him should not perish, but have everlasting life.

For God sent not his Son into the world to condemn the world; but that the world through him might be saved.

John 3:14-19

And as Moses lifted up the serpent in the wilderness, even so must the Son of man be lifted up:

That whosoever believeth in him should not perish, but have eternal life.

For God so loved the world, that he gave his only begotten Son, that whosoever believeth in him should not perish, but have everlasting life.

For God sent not his Son into the world to condemn the world; but that the world through him might be saved.

He that believeth on him is not condemned: but he that believeth not is condemned already, because he hath not believed in the name of the only begotten Son of God.

And this is the condemnation, that light is come into the world, and men loved darkness rather than light, because their deeds were evil.

Psalm 34:8-19

O taste and see that the LORD *is* good: blessed *is* the man *that* trusteth in him.

O fear the LORD, ye his saints: for *there is* no want to them that fear him.

The young lions do lack, and suffer hunger: but they that seek the LORD shall not want any good *thing.*

Come, ye children, hearken unto me: I will teach you the fear of the LORD.

What man *is he that* desireth life, *and* loveth *many* days, that he may see good?

Keep thy tongue from evil, and thy lips from speaking guile.

Depart from evil, and do good; seek peace, and pursue it.

The eyes of the LORD *are* upon the righteous, and his ears *are open* unto their cry.

The face of the LORD *is* against them that do evil, to cut off the remembrance of them from the earth.

The righteous cry, and the LORD heareth, and delivereth them out of all their troubles.

The LORD *is* nigh unto them that are of a broken heart; and saveth such as be of a contrite spirit.

Many *are* the afflictions of the righteous: but the LORD delivereth him out of them all.

Proverbs 3:5-6

Trust in the LORD with all thine heart; and lean not unto thine own understanding.

In all thy ways acknowledge him, and he shall direct thy paths.

Romans 10:9

That if thou shalt confess with thy mouth the Lord Jesus, and shalt believe in thine heart that God hath raised him from the dead, thou shalt be saved.

Matthew 18:1-6

At the same time came the disciples unto Jesus, saying, Who is the greatest in the kingdom of heaven?

And Jesus called a little child unto him, and set him in the midst of them,

And said, Verily I say unto you, Except ye be converted, and become as little children, ye shall not enter into the kingdom of heaven.

Whosoever therefore shall humble himself as this little child, the same is greatest in the kingdom of heaven.

And whoso shall receive one such little child in my name receiveth me.

But whoso shall offend one of these little ones which believe in me, it were better for him that a millstone were hanged about his neck, and *that* he were drowned in the depth of the sea.

Matthew 11:28-30

Come unto me, all ye that labour and are heavy laden, and I will give you rest.

Take my yoke upon you, and learn of me; for I am meek and lowly in heart: and ye shall find rest unto your souls.

For my yoke *is* easy, and my burden is light.

Matthew 22:36-39

Master, which *is* the great command-ment in the law?

Jesus said unto him, Thou shalt love the Lord thy God with all thy heart, and with all thy soul, and with all thy mind.

This is the first and great commandment.

And the second *is* like unto it, Thou shalt love thy neighbour as thyself.

Genesis 1:1-5

In the beginning God created the heaven and the earth.

And the earth was without form, and void; and darkness *was* upon the face of the deep. And the Spirit of God moved upon the face of the waters.

And God said, Let there be light: and there was light.

And God saw the light, that *it was* good: and God divided the light from the darkness.

And God called the light Day, and the darkness he called Night. And the evening and the morning were the first day.

John 14:1-6

Let not your heart be troubled: ye believe in God, believe also in me.

In my Father's house are many mansions: if *it were* not *so*, I would have told you. I go to prepare a place for you.

And if I go and prepare a place for you, I will come again, and receive you unto myself; that where I am, *there* ye may be also.

And whither I go ye know, and the way ye know.

Thomas saith unto him, Lord, we know not whither thou goest; and how can we know the way?

Jesus saith unto him, I am the way, the truth, and the life: no man cometh unto the Father, but by me.

Matthew 5:13-16

Ye are the salt of the earth: but if the salt have lost his savour, wherewith shall it be salted? it is thenceforth good for nothing, but to be cast out, and to be trodden under foot of men.

Ye are the light of the world. A city that is set on an hill cannot be hid.

Neither do men light a candle, and put it under a bushel, but on a candlestick; and it giveth light unto all that are in the house.

Let your light so shine before men, that they may see your good works, and glorify your Father which is in heaven.

Luke 2:8-14

And there were in the same country shepherds abiding in the field, keeping watch over their flock by night.

And, lo, the angel of the Lord came upon them, and the glory of the Lord shone round about them: and they were sore afraid.

And the angel said unto them, Fear not: for, behold, I bring you good tidings of great joy, which shall be to all people.

For unto you is born this day in the city of David a Saviour, which is Christ the Lord.

And this *shall* be a sign unto you; Ye shall find the babe wrapped in swaddling clothes, lying in a manger.

And suddenly there was with the angel a multitude of the heavenly host praising God, and saying,

Glory to God in the highest, and on earth peace, good will toward men.

 Psalm 1

Blessed *is* the man that walketh not in the counsel of the ungodly, nor standeth in the way of sinners, nor sitteth in the seat of the scornful.

But his delight *is* in the law of the LORD; and in his law doth he meditate day and night.

And he shall be like a tree planted by the rivers of water, that bringeth forth his fruit in his season; his leaf also shall not wither; and whatsoever he doeth shall prosper.

The ungodly *are* not so: but *are* like the chaff which the wind driveth away.

Therefore the ungodly shall not stand in the judgment, nor sinners in the congregation of the righteous.

For the LORD knoweth the way of the righteous: but the way of the ungodly shall perish.

Psalm 24

The earth *is* the LORD's, and the fulness thereof; the world, and they that dwell therein.

For he hath founded it upon the seas, and established it upon the floods.

Who shall ascend into the hill of the LORD? or who shall stand in his holy place?

He that hath clean hands, and a pure heart; who hath not lifted up his soul unto vanity, nor sworn deceitfully.

He shall receive the blessing from the LORD, and righteousness from the God of his salvation.

This *is* the generation of them that seek him, that seek thy face, O Jacob. Selah.

Lift up your heads, O ye gates; and be ye lift up, ye everlasting doors; and the King of glory shall come in.

Who *is* this King of glory? The LORD strong and mighty, the LORD mighty in battle.

Lift up your heads, O ye gates; even lift *them* up, ye everlasting doors; and the King of glory shall come in.

Who is this King of glory? The LORD of hosts, he *is* the King of glory. Selah.

Matthew 5:3-12

Blessed *are* the poor in spirit: for theirs is the kingdom of heaven.

Blessed *are* they that mourn: for they shall be comforted.

Blessed *are* the meek: for they shall inherit the earth.

Blessed *are* they which do hunger and thirst after righteousness: for they shall be filled.

Blessed *are* the merciful: for they shall obtain mercy.

Blessed *are* the pure in heart: for they shall see God.

Blessed *are* the peacemakers: for they shall be called the children of God.

Blessed *are* they which are persecuted for righteousness' sake: for theirs is the kingdom of heaven.

Blessed are ye, when *men* shall revile you, and persecute *you,* and shall say all manner of evil against you falsely, for my sake.

Rejoice, and be exceeding glad: for great *is* your reward in heaven: for so persecuted they the prophets which were before you.

Hebrews 11:1-6

Now faith is the substance of things hoped for, the evidence of things not seen.

For by it the elders obtained a good report.

Through faith we understand that the worlds were framed by the word of God, so that things which are seen were not made of things which do appear.

By faith Abel offered unto God a more excellent sacrifice than Cain, by which he obtained witness that he was righteous, God testifying of his gifts: and by it he being dead yet speaketh.

By faith Enoch was translated that he should not see death; and was not found, because God had translated him: for before his translation he had this testimony, that he pleased God.

But without faith *it is* impossible to please *him:* for he that cometh to God must believe that he is, and *that* he is a rewarder of them that diligently seek him.

Hebrews 11:7-10

By faith Noah, being warned of God of things not seen as yet, moved with fear, prepared an ark to the saving of his house; by the which he condemned the world, and became heir of the righteousness which is by faith.

By faith Abraham, when he was called to go out into a place which he should after receive for an inheritance, obeyed; and he went out, not knowing whither he went.

By faith he sojourned in the land of promise, as *in* a strange country, dwelling in tabernacles with Isaac and Jacob, the heirs with him of the same promise:

For he looked for a city which hath foundations, whose builder and maker *is* God.

Hebrews 11:11-15

Through faith also Sara herself received strength to conceive seed, and was delivered of a child when she was past age, because she judged him faithful who had promised.

Therefore sprang there even of one, and him as good as dead, *so many* as the stars of the sky in multitude, and as the sand which is by the sea shore innumerable.

These all died in faith, not having received the promises, but having seen them afar off, and were persuaded of *them,* and embraced *them,* and confessed that they were strangers and pilgrims on the earth.

For they that say such things declare plainly that they seek a country.

And truly, if they had been mindful of that *country* from whence they came out, they might have had opportunity to have returned.

Hebrews 11:16-19

But now they desire a better *country,* that is, an heavenly: wherefore God is not ashamed to be called their God: for he hath prepared for them a city.

By faith Abraham, when he was tried, offered up Isaac: and he that had received the promises offered up his only begotten *son.*

Of whom it was said, That in Isaac shall thy seed be called:

Accounting that God *was* able to raise *him* up, even from the dead; from whence also he received him in a figure.

Hebrews 11:20-22

By faith Isaac blessed Jacob and Esau concerning things to come.

By faith Jacob, when he was a dying, blessed both the sons of Joseph; and worshipped, *leaning* upon the top of his staff.

By faith Joseph, when he died, made mention of the departing of the children of Israel; and gave commandment concerning his bones.

Hebrews 11:23-26

By faith Moses, when he was born, was hid three months of his parents, because they saw *he was* a proper child; and they were not afraid of the king's commandment.

By faith Moses, when he was come to years, refused to be called the son of Pharaoh's daughter;

Choosing rather to suffer affliction with the people of God, than to enjoy the pleasures of sin for a season;

Esteeming the reproach of Christ greater riches than the treasures in Egypt: for he had respect unto the recompence of the reward.

Hebrews 11:27-30

By faith he forsook Egypt, not fearing the wrath of the king: for he endured, as seeing him who is invisible.

Through faith he kept the passover, and the sprinkling of blood, lest he that destroyed the firstborn should touch them.

By faith they passed through the Red sea as by dry *land:* which the Egyptians assaying to do were drowned.

By faith the walls of Jericho fell down, after they were compassed about seven days.

Hebrews 11:31-34

By faith the harlot Rahab perished not with them that believed not, when she had received the spies with peace.

And what shall I more say? for the time would fail me to tell of Gideon, and *of* Barak, and *of* Samson, and *of* Jeph´-thae; *of* David also, and Samuel, and *of* the prophets:

Who through faith subdued kingdoms, wrought righteousness, obtained promises, stopped the mouths of lions,

Quenched the violence of fire, escaped the edge of the sword, out of weakness were made strong, waxed valiant in fight, turned to flight the armies of the aliens.

Hebrews 11:35-38

Women received their dead raised to life again: and others were tortured, not accepting deliverance; that they might obtain a better resurrection:

And others had trial of *cruel* mockings and scourgings, yea, moreover of bonds and imprisonment:

They were stoned, they were sawn asunder, were tempted, were slain with the sword: they wandered about in sheepskins and goatskins; being destitute, afflicted, tormented;

(Of whom the world was not worthy:) they wandered in deserts, and *in* mountains, and *in* dens and caves of the earth.

Hebrews 11:39-40

And these all, having obtained a good report through faith, received not the promise:

God having provided some better thing for us, that they without us should not be made perfect.